OLD FATHER TIME

First presented at the Queen's Theatre, Hornchurch, on the 20th December 1976, with the following cast of characters:

Old Father Time	Brian Hewlett
Mrs Sparkle, a charlady	Penny Jones
Dodger, a gypsy busker	Mike Maynard
Bodger, his son	David Brenchley
The Flying Sauceress	Sue Lynne
Watchdog	
A German Tourist	Pauline Lewis
Sergeant Watchit	
A Caveman	
A Beefeater	Tony Stephens
The Dinosaur	
An American Tourist	Sue Beresford
The Prime Minister	
Head Caveman	
Head of the Yeomen of the Guard	Philip Newman
A Japanese Tourist	
A Caveman	
Guy Fawkes	
A Window Cleaner	Don Dryden
Admiral of the Fleet	
A German Tourist	
A Conspirator	
A Caveman	
A Postman	Jeremy Roberts
The Lord Mayor	
An American Tourist	
A Cavewoman	
A Conspirator	
A Road Sweeper	Alison Robertson
Lady Mayoress	

	Jane Alder
	Jacqueline Boivin
	Ben Hole
Tourists, party guests, etc.,	Lisa Hughes
New Father Time, Puppy Watchdog	Wendy Jackson
	Alison McGuire
	Deborah Sinclair
	Frances Smith

The play directed by John Hole
Settings by David Knapman

The action takes place at the Palace of Westminster; inside the top of Big Ben; opposite the Tower of London; and in Space

Time—the present, to start with at any rate

Companies who require a large cast production could use up to thirty actors; but in the original production a cast of twelve, doubling or trebling, was used as shown in the cast list

MUSICAL NUMBERS

ACT I

1	**London, Wonderful London**	Sergeant Watchit, Mrs Sparkle, Press Photographer, Tourists
2	**Two-Man Busker Band**	Dodger and Bodger
3	**Old Father Time**	Mrs Sparkle, Sergeant Watchit, Dodger, Bodger and Company
4	**My Almanac,** incorporating **Mirabile Dictu** (formula)	Old Father Time, Mrs Sparkle, Sergeant Watchit, Dodger, Bodger and Watchdog
5	**Destination Earth**	Flying Sauceress
6	**The Flying Sauceress's Apprentice's Assistant**	Flying Sauceress, Dodger and Bodger
7	**Mirabile Dictu** (formula)	Bodger

ACT II

8	**UG!**	Head Caveman, three Cavemen, Cavewoman
8A	**Mirabile Dictu** (formula)—reprise	Mrs Sparkle
9	**Prehistoric Pet**	Old Father Time, Mrs Sparkle, Watchdog, Dinosaur
9A	**Mirabile Dictu** (formula)—reprise	Old Father Time
10	**Through the Fourth Dimension**	Old Father Time, Mrs Sparkle, Watchdog, Dinosaur (with almanac), with Flying Sauceress, Dodger and Bodger on Saucer
11	**Mumble, Mutter, Murmur**	Guy Fawkes, four Conspirators (including Dodger and Bodger)
11A	**Mirabile Dictu** (formula)—reprise	Old Father Time
11B	**Through the Fourth Dimension—** reprise	Old Father Time, Mrs Sparkle, Watchdog, Dinosaur
11C	**Mirabile Dictu** (formula)—reprise	Flying Sauceress
12	**Auld Lang Syne** (song sheet)	The Company (apart from the Flying Sauceress) and audience
12A	**Old Father Time**—reprise	The Company (apart from the Flying Sauceress)

OLD FATHER TIME

A Family Musical

Book, music and lyrics
by
DAVID WOOD

SAMUEL FRENCH

LONDON
NEW YORK SYDNEY TORONTO
HOLLYWOOD

To AUJ
with love and thanks
for all your encouragement and loyalty
over the years

ACT I

SCENE 1

London. A street in Westminster. Eight a.m. on December 30th

The set is a composite one, to which the play will return several times. It should not be too solid, however, as it will need to disappear in sight of the audience, section by section, as we travel back in time. Visible are Big Ben, an arched entrance to the Houses of Parliament (Westminster Hall), a rooftop (practical), a sentry-box and a pillar-box. In Act II a door to the cellars of the Houses of Parliament will be needed; this could be a trap-door in the stage, if there is one. The same trap-door could also be used for the interior Big Ben scenes in both acts. Since the date is December 30th, there could possibly be some Christmas decorations in the street. (See set plans on pages 66–7, also special note on dismantling)

Before the Curtain rises, as the House Lights go down, we hear the introductory chimes of Big Ben—ding, dong, ding, dong. As the CURTAIN rises, music is heard, in time with which we hear eight chimes signifying eight o'clock

Sergeant Watchit is standing in front of his sentry-box. A group of Tourists faces him, turned away from the audience, giving rise to movement and expectant murmurs. Nearby, Mrs Sparkle, with her bucket and mop, is busy polishing the brass of the door leading into the Houses of Parliament. A Press Photographer waits outside, expecting the arrival of the Prime Minister

On the fourth beat of the chimes, Sergeant Watchit coughs to gain attention. On the fifth beat, he starts addressing his audience

Song 1   LONDON, WONDERFUL LONDON

Sergeant Watchit Ladies and gents, your att-
               -ention, please. May I
             Welcome you all to the
             Houses of Parliament.

The music continues as the Tourists applaud, and Sergeant Watchit mimes the start of his lecture. The focus changes to Mrs Sparkle, who starts to sing

Mrs Sparkle   London, wonderful London
             So much to do
             So much to see
             In
             London, wonderful London town
             London's the place for me.

The Tourists turn and become a chorus, the Press Photographer too

All   London, wonderful London
                              So much to do
                              So much to see
                              In
                              London, wonderful London town
                              London's the place to be.

                              Buckingham Palace, British Museum
                              The Embankment after dark
                              Tower of London, National Gallery
                              Marble Arch, Hyde Park.

                              London, wonderful London
                              So much to do
                              So much to see
                              In
                              London, wonderful London town
                              London's the place for me.

The music continues. The Tourists turn to listen to Sergeant Watchit

Sergeant Watchit (*speaking*) Begun in eighteen forty on the site of the old
Palace of Westminster, the Houses of Parliament has the most famous
clock in the world. (*Indicating Big Ben*) When Parliament sits—a flag flies
from Victoria Tower by day and by night a light burns in the St Stephen's
Tower above.

*The music continues, as the Press Photographer suddenly notices something of
interest off*

Press Photographer (*speaking*) Hey! It's the Prime Minister!

General excitement

All   London, wonderful London
                              So much to do
                              So much to see
                              In
                              London, wonderful London town
                              London's the place to be
                              London we all agree
                              London, wonderful London town
                              London's the place to be.

They all get into a good position to see the Prime Minister

   The Prime Minister enters, waving

Sergeant Watchit clears a path towards the arched door

Sergeant Watchit (*to the crowd*) No jostling of the Right Honourable gent,
if you please. (*To the Prime Minister*) Kindly proceed. SIR!

The "Sir!" is exclaimed vehemently as Sergeant Watchit rigidly jumps to attention. It makes the Prime Minister jump

Prime Minister Thank you, Watchit.
Sergeant Watchit Chilly morning, sir.
Prime Minister I beg your pardon?
Sergeant Watchit Bit chilly, sir. Nippy.
Prime Minister Ah. Well, Watchit, that is something I can't make a snap judgement on. But when my colleagues in the Cabinet and I have discussed it thoroughly, I'll come back to you.
Sergeant Watchit Thank you very much. SIR! (*Another loud one*)

The Prime Minister jumps. A Tourist and the Press Photographer flash their cameras. The Prime Minister poses, then waves farewell. Stately music is heard

The Prime Minister goes into the Houses of Parliament

Sergeant Watchit returns to his sentry-box. The crowd disperses, but some remain on stage—Tourists with guide-books, etc. The music changes to "Yo-heave-ho"-type music

Dodger and Bodger enter, dragging their gypsy caravan—one pulling the shafts, the other pushing from behind. The colourful caravan—which is not very big— has written on one side "Dodger and Son", and on the other "Bodger and Father"

Dodger Whoa!

They stop. Dodger looks around happily

At last. London. City of dreams. Fame and fortune. As we tread these pavements paved with gold, I feel like telling the world ...
Bodger Ow, my feet ache.
Dodger (*carried away*) How my feet ache—no! Shut up, Bodger. I feel like telling the world—watch us, world, we're going places.
Bodger I'm going nowhere. My poor feet are killing me.
Dodger Stop rabbiting on about your feet. Savour this historic moment in our careers.
Bodger But, Dad, they ache something horrible. (*He notices the audience*) Ooh.
Dodger So do mine, but I'm not complaining.
Bodger (*whispering*) Dad ...
Dodger Mine ache with pride. They carried me to—(*with reverence*)—London.
Bodger Dad ...
Dodger City of opportunity. Our stairway to the stars!
Bodger Dad, look ...
Dodger Stars of stage, screen and televis—(*he sees the audience*)—oo-er!
Bodger What are they?
Dodger Waxworks?
Bodger No, they're moving, look! And that one's laughing. And that one's eating a sweet. And that one's rustling a book.

Dodger I've got it. (*Excitedly*) London. Tourists. They're tourists. He's rustling his guide-book.

Bodger So?

Dodger They're our first London audience. This is it. The moment we've waited for. Get the props, quick.

Bodger, smiling a glazed smile at the audience, edges to the caravan and goes in to find props, maybe special jackets and hats—plus any musical instruments the Buskers can play. Meanwhile Dodger makes his introduction
Ladies and Gentlemen, boys and girls—good morning.

After the audience's first response, which will be pretty feeble—

They're all foreigners!

Audience participation to get a decent reaction

Today we are privileged to impress you, our first London audience, with our travelling show. May I introduce the act: buskers, street entertainers extraordinary—(*indicating the side of the caravan*)—Dodger—(*indicating himself*)—and Son.

A chord of music. Dodger works to get applause. The Tourists on the stage begin to take an interest. As Dodger is about to continue, Bodger comes from the caravan, in costume, banging a drum or making some kind of "roll up" sound. Dodger quickly prepares himself for the act

Bodger Ladies and Gentlemen, boys and girls. Good morning.

Audience Good morning.

Bodger Today we are privileg ...vilifrig ...fullofveg ... happy to—er—er ...

Dodger (*prompting, whispering*) Impress you.

Bodger Undress you.

Dodger No!

Bodger No!

Dodger Golly, you're stupid.

Bodger (*to the audience, loudly*) Golly, you're stupid.

Dodger No!

Bodger No!

Dodger Apologize.

Bodger (*to Dodger*) I'm sorry.

Dodger Not to me! To them!

Bodger (*to the audience*) I'm sorry.

Dodger (*interrupting*) Ladies and Gentlemen, boys and girls, presenting, for your edification and delight, the two and only ...

Bodger (*turning the caravan round to show the writing on the other side*) Bodger—(*indicating himself*)—and Father!

During the song Dodger and Bodger employ any skills they have musically, plus juggling, acrobatics, dancing, etc. If one could be a kind of one-man band, it would be very effective

Song 2   TWO-MAN BUSKER BAND

Dodger	One
	Two
	Three
	Four
Bodger	Five
	Six
	Nine
	Eleven

Dodger gives Bodger a crushing look

Dodger ⎱   We are the Two-Man Busker Band   ⎱ *Singing*
Bodger ⎰   The Two-Man Dodger and Bodger Busker Band   ⎰ *together*
                    Sunshine or rain
                    We entertain
                    Singing for our supper ...

By this time the song appears to be going well. The spectators on the stage are reacting favourably, clapping in rhythm, etc. Suddenly there is an interruption, as—

The Prime Minister storms in from the arched entrance

Prime Minister Quiet. Qui——et.

The song grinds to a halt

That's better. You will kindly cease this cacophony forthwith.
Bodger We weren't cacoffeephoning, whatever that means, and we won't cease forthwith. Or fifthwith. So there. (*He puts out his tongue*)
Dodger Bodger. Manners.
Prime Minister Clear off—you—gypsies.
Dodger How dare you!
Prime Minister Busking is against the law. Clear off.
Dodger We're only trying to make people happy ...
Mrs Sparkle Give 'em a chance, Prime Minister.
Prime Minister What?
Mrs Sparkle Give 'em a chance to make people happy.
Prime Minister Shall I?
Audience Yes!
Prime Minister What! Let them do their act now?
Audience Yes.
Prime Minister Oh, very well. Carry on. And if you make *everybody* happy I'll give you a special licence to perform anywhere in London.

Applause. The song continues

Song 2   TWO-MAN BUSKER BAND [*reprise*]

Dodger	One
	Two

                    Three
                    Four
Bodger   Ooh me poor old feet are sore.

Dodger looks witheringly at Bodger

Dodger   We are the Two-Man Busker Band   } *Singing*
Bodger   The Two-Man Dodger and Bodger Busker Band   { *together*
                    Sunshine or rain
                    We entertain
                    Singing for our supper all over the land.
                    We are the Two-Man Busker Band
                    And the busking happy-go-lucky life is grand.
                    Let us brighten your day
                    You don't have to pay
                    To hear the Two-Man Busker Band.

                    Bashing out the rhythm on the big bass drum
                    Singing the kind of songs that people like to hum
                    Dodger and Bodger
                    Two-man travelling show
                    Just step up on the pavement now
                    And listen to us go!

            Short musical virtuosity section

All   They/We are the Two-Man Busker Band
                    The Two-Man Dodger and Bodger Busker Band
                    Sunshine or rain
                    They/We entertain
                    Singing for our supper all over the land.
                    They/We are the Two-Man Busker Band
                    And the busking happy-go-lucky life is grand
                    Let us brighten your day
                    You don't have to pay
                    To hear the Two-Man Busker Band.

Dodger } We don't need a microphone or studio   } *Singing*
Bodger { We can make music live in any place we go   { *together*
                    Bet you we'll get you
                    Tap tap tapping your feet
                    And by the second chorus
                    You'll be dancing in the street.

            Musical virtuosity section

This continues as long as practicable, using as many different sounds, etc. as possible

Dodger   Come on
                    Set your feet a-tapping

The audience is encouraged to participate

Bodger   Get your fingers snapping

Dodger ⎱ Swing to the right   ⎰ *Singing*
Bodger ⎰ And the left   ⎱ *together*
              And the right

              La la la the chorus
              With all of your might.

Audience participation: "La la la" chorus

              Let us brighten your day
              You don't have to pay
              To hear the Two-Man Busker Band.

              We may not be the Philharmonic
              But we guarantee a real good tonic
              The Two-Man Busker Band.

              Short section of musical virtuosity

              Mornings, ev'nings, afternoons
Dodger   I play the tunes
Bodger   And I play the spoons.
Dodger ⎱ The Two-Man Busker Band   ⎰ *Singing*
Bodger ⎰ So give a big hand   ⎱ *together*
              To the Two-Man Busker Band.

At the end of the song Bodger returns inside the caravan. Dodger takes one of the spoons he has been playing

Dodger Prime Minister, Ladies and Gentlemen, boys and girls. Mind over matter. One ordinary silver spoon. Courtesy of British Rail. Before your astonished eyes I will cause it to bend to an angle of ninety degrees. Thank you. (*He prepares himself, then stops*) Can you all see? Not really? Very well. (*He goes to the caravan and produces a very large spoon, three or four feet long*)

Music for atmosphere

Dodger holds the spoon in the centre with one hand, and rubs the stem near the bowl with the other. Tortured grimaces of concentration. Eventually the other end—furthest from the bowl—bends. Dodger is intently watching the bowl end and does not notice until the last moment. (This should be based on the old panto-mime gag of sawing one end of a piece of wood, and the other end falling off.) The crowd applauds. Dodger bows

Prime Minister Well, what does everyone think? Did they make you happy?
Audience Yes!
Prime Minister Very well. Here you are. (*He hands Dodger a licence*)
All Hooray!
Mrs Sparkle Three cheers for the Prime Minister. Hip, hip—
All Hooray.
Mrs Sparkle Hip hip—

All Hooray.
Mrs Sparkle Hip hip—
All Hooray.
Mrs Sparkle He's a real heaven sent.
Prime Minister Heaven sent?
Mrs Sparkle A real GENT! (*Explaining*) Heaven sent—gent.
Prime Minister (*bemused*) Oh. Thank you.

The Prime Minister exits. Bodger returns.

Mrs Sparkle comes forward. She carries her mop and bucket. She goes to Bodger and Dodger

And you two are real chunky! Got me plates of meat going.
Bodger (*bewildered*) Did we? Dad, we got her plates of meat going.
Dodger Good. (*Whispering*) What's she talking about?
Mrs Sparkle (*laughing*) Sorry, dearie, it's the Cockney rhyming slang. Plates of meat—(*she encourages the audience to "translate"*)—FEET! You'll have to learn all that now you're staying in London. Listen, how do you fancy a nice cup of Rosie Lee?
Bodger Who?
Mrs Sparkle Rosie Lee—(*she waits for the audience to "translate"*)—TEA!
Dodger Tea?
Mrs Sparkle You've got to keep your strength up. When did you last eat?
Bodger When we had our horse.
Mrs Sparkle You ate your horse?
Bodger No. We last ate when we had him but we had to sell him because we couldn't afford to keep him.
Mrs Sparkle That settles it. You're coming with me. Now, I'm Mrs Sparkle and I work for yer actual Old Father Time. He'll be very chuffed to meet you, I'm sure. Oh Sergeant Watchit!

Sergeant Watchit comes forward

Sergeant Watchit Sir! (*He realizes*) I mean—marm!
Mrs Sparkle All right if I take Mr Dodger and Mr Bodger for a cup of Rosie Lee with Old Father Time?
Sergeant Watchit Certainly, Mrs Sparkle. In fact—(*he looks at his watch*)—any moment now ...

A telephone bell rings. Bodger and Dodger look around

Ah! (*He opens a section of his busby, revealing a telephone, and answers it*) Watchit ... Right away, sir ... Thank you. (*He replaces the phone and turns to the others*) As I thought. I may have the pleasure of accompanying you to Old Father Time's office. My security round commences there.
Dodger But who is Old Father Time?
Mrs Sparkle You've never heard of Old Father Time?
Sergeant Watchit He controls every second, every minute, every hour of every day and every night of every week of every month of every year.
Bodger Where does he live?

Mrs Sparkle Use your brains, dearie! What's the ideal London home for the person in charge of time?

Dodger and Bodger cannot think, so Mrs Sparkle turns to the audience. Participation

That's right. Big Ben.

Sergeant Watchit Right at the top.

Mrs Sparkle So, to get there, we have to climb lots and lots of apples and pears.

Dodger
Bodger } Apples and pears?   } *Speaking together*

Mrs Sparkle Apples and pears—(*with the audience*)—STAIRS!

Song 3   OLD FATHER TIME

Mrs Sparkle   ) Old Father Time
Sergeant Watchit } Old Father Time
Chorus   ) Old Father Time
                                  Old Father Time

Chorus Old Father Time   **Mrs Sparkle**   } Checking his charts
                 Old Father Time   **Sergeant Watchit** } Doing his sums
                 Old Father Time   Making sure
                 Old Father Time   Tomorrow comes
                 When you hear   Day after day
                   Big Ben chime   Night after night
                 Hear Big Ben chime   Making sure
                 Hear Big Ben chime   They turn out right
                 And you know it's   He's been around
                 Old Father Time.   Since time's beginning
                                                                                    Making sure
                                                                                    The world keeps spinning
                                                                                    Big Ben will always chime
                                                                                    As long as there's a Father Time.

All   The setting of the sun
                          The rising of the moon
                          The moment when a morning
                          Becomes an afternoon

He monitors each minute
As the clock ticks by
When season follows season
He's the reason why.

Half   } Old Father Time
Chorus } Old Father Time
Old Father Time
Old Father Time
When you hear
  Big Ben chime
Hear Big Ben chime
Hear Big Ben chime
And you know it's
Father Time.

Half   } Checking his charts
Chorus } Doing his sums
Making sure
Tomorrow comes
Day after day
Night after night
Making sure
They turn out right
He's been around
Since time's begin-
  ning
Making sure
The   world   keeps
  spinning
Big Ben will always
  chime
As long as there's a
Father Time.

All   The very first hallo
The very last good-bye
The moment when a chrys'lis
Becomes a butterfly
He's checking ev'ry second
As the clock ticks by
When Monday follows Sunday
He's the reason why.

Half   } Old Father Time
Chorus } Old Father Time
Old Father Time
Old Father Time
When you hear
  Big Ben chime
Hear Big Ben chime
Hear Big Ben chime
And you know it's
Old Father Time
Old Father Time.

Half   } Checking his charts
Chorus } Doing his sums
Making sure
Tomorrow comes
Day after day
Night after night
Making sure
They turn out right
He's been around
Since time's begin-
  ning
Making sure
The   world   keeps
  spinning

> Big Ben will always
> chime
> As long as there's a
> Father Time
> Old Father Time
> Old Father Time.

Towards the end of the song the set begins to change to—

SCENE 2

At the top of Big Ben

This is the office and living accommodation of Old Father Time. The window is one of the huge clock-faces of Big Ben. The hands will have to be practical, or at least able to be moved to different positions. They are now approaching nine o'clock. Incorporated in the window, possibly one of the latticed sections, is a door which leads out to a ledge. A large calendar takes up considerable wall space. It shows December, with all dates up and including the 28th crossed off. Various dials, cog-wheels and other pieces of mechanism are visible, together with a desk with flashing lights and a microphone. This is Old Father Time's console, with which he keeps in contact with the world of time. Also in sight are his traditional hour-glass and sickle. The main door to the room is, if possible, a trap-door in the centre of the floor. This would give the impression that, to reach it, one has to climb stairs up a high tower. (This is not essential, however.) Another exit is marked "To the Main Cog". To one side is a kennel in the shape of a cuckoo-clock, and fairly central is Old Father Time's bed. This is made from the shell of an old grandfather clock: the headboard is a large alarm clock with a hammer rigged to strike the occupant of the bed when the alarm goes off

At the end of the previous song, Mrs Sparkle, Sergeant Watchit, Dodger and Bodger exit. If the arched entrance is still visible, they go through it: if not, they simply move off the stage, leaving behind them the top of Big Ben set in position

Old Father Time, in white gown and nightcap, is fast asleep in bed. After a couple of snores, the alarm bell rings violently and the hammer clunks down on Old Father Time's head. Then it goes rhythmically up and down. Old Father Time wakes up and tries to get up, but each time is knocked down by the hammer. Eventually he reaches the mechanism that controls both alarm and hammer, and stops them. All the time there can be background clock noises. Very meticulously, Old Father Time sits up, pushes the sheet back, and rolls or folds up his very long beard. Then he swings his long-john-clad legs out of bed. Suddenly he notices the audience

Old Father Time Good gracious! (*He pulls his nightgown over his legs to regain* *his modesty. This necessitates leaving go of his beard, which unrolls. To the audience, embarrassed)* Good Morning.

Audience Good morning.

Old Father Time Didn't know you were coming. Caught me off guard. (*He stands and trips over his beard*) Drat and double drat. (*To the audience*) Oh, I beg your pardon, but the older I get the more stupid I get, yet the older I get the more work I have to do. To prepare the way for the new Father Time. Look. (*He goes to the calendar and crosses off the 29th of December*) Today's the thirtieth. In thirty-nine hours eight minutes and twenty seconds precisely, I retire! Midnight of New Year's Eve. And Watchdog ret . . . have you met Watchdog?

Audience No.

Old Father Time He's probably still asleep, then. (*He goes to the kennel*) Watchdog! (*No reaction*) Doggie Woggie Watchdog! (*No reaction*) He's flat out. You know, that dog would sleep through West Ham scoring the winning goal in the Cup Final. Will you give him a call with me? Thank you. After three—one, two, three . . .

Audience Watchdog!!

Old Father Time bends down to look in the kennel

Suddenly Watchdog pops out and leapfrogs over Old Father Time, knocking him flat, then jumps on him, smothering him with licks and affection

Old Father Time Get off me. Get off! Hopeless hound.

He tries to stand, but is knocked to the ground again by Watchdog, who barks excitedly. Then suddenly Watchdog begins to wind down. His movements become slower and jerky, and his barks, too. He finally comes to a complete halt

Oh good, he's wound down. Clockwork, you see.

He winds up Watchdog with a large key attached to his back. A sound effect accompanies the winding. Watchdog jerks back to life

There's a good boy. Do you want your oil?

Watchdog barks. Old Father Time gives him an oil-can, from which he drinks eagerly

Have to keep his sprockets well lubricated. That better?

Watchdog barks, then points at the clock-face behind

What? Oh, yes. Time's ticking on. Nine o'clock synchronization in five minutes. Check the main cog.

Old Father Time wraps his beard round his neck like a scarf and exits to the main cog

(*As he goes*) Stay here and keep watch, Watchdog.

Watchdog sits near the main entrance. If a stage trap-door is used, we should be unaware it exists until we suddenly hear voices

Sergeant Watchit		Four hundred and	
Mrs Sparkle	*(off, or under)*	eight, four hundred	{ *Speaking*
Dodger		and nine, four	{ *together*
Bodger		hundred and ten ...	

Watchdog barks ferociously and prepares for action. A secret knock on the trap-door is heard. Watchdog opens it a small way and barks: "Password"

| **Mrs Sparkle** | *(off)* | A stitch in time saves | { *Speaking* |
| **Sergeant Watchit** | | eight-and-a-half | { *together* |

Watchdog calms down immediately and opens the door

Sergeant Watchit, Mrs Sparkle, Dodger and Bodger enter. All are a little breathless

Sergeant Watchit Thank you, Watchdog.

Mrs Sparkle Morning, dearie. This is Mr Dodger and Mr Bodger.

Bodger Four hundred and thirteen, four hundred and fourteen, four hundred ... (*He still walks round and round as though up a staircase*)

Dodger Bodger! We've arrived!

Bodger (*in a daze*) Oh, sorry. I've never seen so many apples and pears. Enough to open a greengrocer's.

Old Father Time enters

Watchdog barks a greeting

Old Father Time Morning, Sergeant Watchit. (*He quickly covers his ears with his hands*)

Mrs Sparkle and Watchdog do the same

Sergeant Watchit Good morning. (*Jumping to attention*) SIR!

Dodger and Bodger jump. The others do not, used to this ritual. They remove their hands from their ears

A.M. Security check, sir, checking your security this A.M.

Old Father Time All's well, Sergeant. Relax.

Sergeant Watchit sits down

Mrs Sparkle 'Scuse me, Father Time, dearie.

Old Father Time Mrs Sparkle. (*He sees Dodger and Bodger*) Oh, good morning.

Mrs Sparkle I hope it's all right. I've invited these two busker gentlemen for a cup of Rosie Lee. They do a lovely show in the street.

Dodger How so, sir? Dodger's the name.

Old Father Time Really? What do you dodge?

Bodger Rotten eggs and tomatoes, mainly.

Dodger Bodger! My son, sir, Bodger; so called because he always does things wrong.

Bodger How do? (*He comes forward to shake hands, trips, and falls flat on his face*)

Dodger See what I mean?
Old Father Time Put the kettle on, Mrs Sparkle.
Mrs Sparkle Do you think it'll suit me? Ha, ha. Thank you, dearie. Cuppa
    for you, Sergeant?
Sergeant Watchit Most kind, marm. (*He sits again*)

*Mrs Sparkle goes to prepare tea. Bodger starts wandering round looking at
things. Watchdog eyes him. Old Father Time prepares a few switches at his console: towards the end of his next speech Bodger picks up a large red tome*

Dodger. What an amazing room this is, sir.
Old Father Time Is it? Yes, I suppose it is, really. Most people don't believe
    it exists. Not surprising, though. Most people don't believe *I* exist. But some-
    one has to look after time or anything might happen....

Seeing Bodger with the tome, Watchdog barks

    DON'T TOUCH THAT!

*Bodger drops the book. Old Father Time rushes to it and holds it carefully, hoping
it is all right*

Bodger I'm sorry. What is it?
Old Father Time It's a very special book.

Song 4   MY ALMANAC

Old Father Time An almanac, Bodger, my almanac, Dodger
               The principal reason for Watchit's patrol.

Sergeant Watchit (*speaking*) Watchit by name, watch it by nature—(*loudly*)—
    Sir!

All jump. Old Father Time continues his song, opening the almanac

Old Father Time In this tome are the secrets of time, how it works
               All its myst'ries revealed, its rhythms and quirks
               And the formulas for its control.
               I would be lost
               Without this mystic book
               And no-one else
               Is allowed to look.

Mrs Sparkle ⎫
             ⎬ Allowed to look.   ⎧ *Singing*
Sergeant Watchit ⎭   ⎨ *together*

*Old Father Time snaps the almanac shut, as Dodger and Bodger try to nose
a glimpse*

Old Father Time   But
                  If, alas and alack,
                  I lost my almanac
                  I'd lose all track
                  I'd lose my knack

My nerve would crack
I'd get the sack
So should some charlatan quack
Attack my almanac
I would stop at nothing
To get it back.

Mrs Sparkle } If alas and alack   } *Singing*
Sergeant Watchit } He lost his almanac   } *together*
He'd lose all track
He'd lose his knack
His nerve would crack
He'd get the sack
So should some charlatan quack
Attack his almanac
He would stop at nothing
To get it back.

Old Father Time Suppose, as a game, that you mentioned my name
To the average man in the average street
He'd say "Who?—Oh, I know, he's that bloke with a beard
He's around at New Year, he looks a bit weird
'Cos he's always wrapped up in a sheet."
I could get by
Without my beard or sheet
Those aren't the things
That make me complete.

Mrs Sparkle } Make him complete.   } *Singing*
Sergeant Watchit }   } *together*

All, including   But
Dodger and   If alas and alack
Bodger   I/He lost my/his almanac
I'd/He'd lost all track
I'd/He'd lost my/his knack
My/His nerve would crack
I'd/He'd get the sack
So should some charlatan quack
Attack my/his almanac
I/He would stop at nothing
To get it back.

The music continues under the dialogue

Old Father Time Now, there's just time for a demonstration. Interested?
Dodger Of course, sir. What can the almanac do?
Old Father Time Let's find a formula. Any page at random. (*He lets the almanac fall open*) Here we are. Action replay.
Bodger Action replay?

Old Father Time Yes. Now, you do something from your act and I'll chant
the formula for a replay, holding on to the almanac—that's vital! Then see
what happens.

*Dodger and Bodger get in a huddle and decide what to do. It should preferably
be something energetic or acrobatic, which takes them from one side of the stage
to the other. Drum roll. They perform their trick, ending with a flourish, arms
outstretched*

(*Chanting from the almanac*) Mirabile dictu orbe tum
                                                  Recantate hac actionem nunc ipsum.

*There is a loud electronic noise, during which the power of the formula forces
the surprised Dodger and Bodger back to their starting place. Drum roll. Dodger
and Bodger repeat their performance. As they finish, they look amazed*

(*Speaking*) Correct to norm! The Action Replay! (*He takes a bow*)

Dodger, Bodger and Mrs Sparkle applaud. The song continues

(*Singing*)   I'm often depicted, my movement restricted
                           By objects I clutch as my symbols of power

*Mrs Sparkle and Sergeant Watchit fetch the sickle and hour-glass and put them
in his hands*

                           In my left hand a sickle, in the right an hour-glass
                           Through the centre of which the sands of time pass
                           But they can't tell the date or the hour.
                           I could get by
                           Without a grain of sand
                           Sand doesn't help
                           Me to understand.

Mrs Sparkle
Sergeant Watchit } To understand   { *Singing*
Dodger   { *together*
Bodger

Old Father Time ⎞ But
Mrs Sparkle   ⎟ If alas and alack
Sergeant Watchit ⎬ I/He lost my/his almanac
Dodger   ⎟ I'd/He'd lose all track
Bodger   ⎠ I'd/He'd lose my/his knack
                              My/his nerve would crack
                              I'd/He'd get the sack
                              So should some charlatan quack
                              Attack my/his almanac
                              I/He would stop at nothing

Mrs Sparkle
Sergeant Watchit } And neither would we
Dodger
Bodger

Old Father Time	I would stop at nothing
Mrs Sparkle	
Sergeant Watchit	Just try it and see
Dodger	
Bodger	

Old Father Time   The loss of my sickle
                      Wouldn't put me in a pickle
All   But I/he would stop at nothing
                      To get my/his almanac
                      Back!

At the end of the song there is a whistling sound

Old Father Time What on earth . . . ?

Old Father Time and Watchdog rush to check dials, etc. All look anxious

Mrs Sparkle Ooh. I completely forgot. It's my kettle!

Relief. Mrs Sparkle goes to make the tea

Old Father Time (*calling*) You won't forget about tomorrow, will you, Mrs Sparkle?

Mrs Sparkle No, of course not, dearie. (*Arriving with the tray*) What's happening tomorrow?

Old Father Time New Year's Eve. The change-over. You will make sure everything's really spick and span for the new Father Time?

Mrs Sparkle Need you ask, dearie? Just like I done it for you! This time last year. (*She hands out tea*)

Old Father Time And food for the party. Aha, I've had an idea. Dodger and Bodger could entertain at the party!

Enthusiastic response from the others. Mrs Sparkle starts cleaning with her mop and bucket

Dodger We'd be honoured, sir.

Watchdog starts barking furiously from the console, pointing at the clock-face, which says very nearly nine o'clock

Old Father Time Ah, good gracious. Nine o'clock synchronization. (*He rushes to the console and puts on headphones*)

Watchdog does the same

    (*To the others*) You can watch if you like, but I warn you, it gets pretty noisy. (*He turns a knob*)

Electronic noises. Lights flash. Then Old Father Time speaks into a microphone. Throughout this section he twiddles knobs, checks dials, etc., and consults the almanac

    Father Time calling. Father Time calling. Thirty seconds to nine o'clock sync. Greenwich Mean Time come in, please. Over.

Garbled Radio Voice Greenwich receiving you. Standing by with pips. Over.

Old Father Time Independent Radio News. Come in, please. Over.

Garbled Radio Voice Thank you, Father Time. I.R.N. receiving. Over.
Old Father Time B.B.C., B.B.C., come in, please. Eighteen seconds to nine
  o'clock sync. Over.
Garbled Radio Voice B.B.C. receiving you loud and clear. Over.
Old Father Time Big Ben introductory chimes—GO!

*The chimes preceding the single clangs start. They are quite loud. The spectators
cover their ears with their hands (but the audience should not be encouraged to
do this in case they miss the action!) Half-way through the chimes Old Father
Time speaks*

Old Father Time Greenwich Mean Time. Stand by with pips. And GO!

*The six Greenwich pips start. On the sixth, the first booming Big Ben clang starts,
followed by eight more*

  (*During the strike*) I.R.N. and B.B.C. stand by for news bulletins—(*just after
  the last clang*)—GO!
Radio Voice 1 ⎫ Good morning and welcome to the latest news ⎧*Speaking*
             ⎬ from I.R.N. with the time at nine o'clock ... ⎨
Radio Voice 2 ⎭ It's nine o'clock. This is B.B.C. Radio Four. And ⎩*together*
             here is the news ...

*Old Father Time clicks off a switch, turning off the I.R.N. voice. The B.B.C.
voice continues*

Radio Voice 2 A disturbing report that an Unidentified Flying Object has been
  spotted over London. A spokesman from the Air Ministry roof reports that
  first sightings indicate a saucer-like object which hovers over the City, then
  speeds up into the clouds. This leads experts to suppose that the spaceship,
  or whatever it is, intends to land.

*Dramatic chord. All look at one another, concerned, as the Lights fade to a
Black-out*

SCENE 3

*A strange, eerie electronic noise echoes from the blackness. This sound is impor-
tant, as it becomes the recognizable "signature tune" heralding the arrival of
the Flying Sauceress, and later the audience will react simply to the noise*

*A flying saucer, lit perhaps by ultra-violet light and on a revolving black tower,
appears to be suspended in mid-air. (This system might also be made to work
by using a narrow follow-spot.) On the saucer sits the Flying Sauceress, an ele-
gant green invader from outer space*

Song 5   DESTINATION EARTH

Flying Sauceress (*singing*)
  Careering through the cosmos like a meteor in flight
  Streaking through the stratosphere at twice the speed of light

Skimming the horizon at an ultrasonic pace
Flashing through the firmament, the Queen of Outer Space.

On my flying saucer
On my flying saucer
Nothing is impossible, no distance is too far
I can travel anywhere on my private shooting star
On my flying saucer
Masterpiece of aviation
Destination
Earth.

A-swooping past the planets, Venus, Mars, the Milky Way
Mistress of the universe I speed towards my prey
Unsuspecting earthlings now prepare to meet your fate
Soon I will be landing, the ambassadress of hate.

On my flying saucer
On my flying saucer
Nothing is impossible, no distance is too far
I can travel anywhere on my private shooting star
On my flying saucer
Miracle of levitation
Destination
Earth
On my flying saucer
On my flying saucer
On my flying saucer.

She becomes aware of the audience. She speaks with little emotion—icy cool

Ah. Earthlings. Unintelligent, unsuspecting earthlings with less brain than
I have in the nail of my little toe. They will soon submit. They will soon
be my slaves. (*Addressing the audience*) Earthlings! Can you hear me? You
can? Then listen to my words. I, the Flying Sauceress, have flown from
my planet Ufrenia, in search of volunteers, you, to come and work for us
in our uranium mines. Seven days a week. Sixteen hours a day. Under-
ground. No luncheon vouchers. Will you come?

The audience should decline

You don't want to work for us?

Again the audience should say "No"

No? You astronomically clueless loonies—you have no choice! I can *make*
you come with me. (*She dramatically produces a ray gun*) See this? One
second of fluence from this ray gun and you will be under my power. One
second's worth and you'll never go home again. Now. (*Looking round*) Who
looks muscular and healthy? Mm, rather a teeny weeny weedy bunch of
specimens, who fidget. Well, you'd better not fidget as I fluence you. Otherwise the fluence cannot squeeze between the cells of your horrid, squirming,
little earthling bodies. So keep still, all of you.

This should encourage the audience to move about. The Flying Sauceress tries to take aim on several of them, but cannot find a still one. She begins to lose her temper

Now, there's a juicy subject. (*She takes aim*) Stop moving. Stop it! Aaah. How about that one! He's not looking. He's still, he's still! Don't you dare tell him! Aah, he's moving. You evil brood of arch-nasties. Very well, if *you* won't co-operate, City of London, citizens of London, here I come. And watch out. If I meet you again and you're not moving, nice and still and unsuspecting, ssssssssss—(*pointing her ray gun*)—and you'll be my slaves! (*She laughs gaily*)

The sound of the flying saucer builds again and she flies away as the Lights fade to a Black-out

SCENE 4

London. The same composite set as Scene 1

The Busker's caravan is at the side of the stage, where it ended up at the end of Scene 1. Dodger and Bodger enter

Bodger Oh Dad, can't we rest a moment? Ooo ...

Dodger ⎫(*mimicking*) My feet ache.   ⎫ *Speaking*
Bodger ⎭   ⎬ *together*
Dodger All right, we can spend the night here, and start work tomorrow—
"London, wonderful London".

Music. Bodger goes into the caravan to fetch an eiderdown. Dodger starts to remove his trousers, remembers the audience, and modestly turns his back. He takes off his trousers. Underneath them he has pyjama trousers, perhaps with "Night Night" written on them

It's all happening for us, Bodger.

The Flying Sauceress enters to roughly the spot where Bodger was. She is not holding the ray gun

The Big Time at last! (*He turns, see the Flying Sauceress and does a huge double-take*) Would you care to sit down, love? You look a bit poorly.

Bodger emerges

Bodger Dad, I .... Oooo, Dad, who's your friend with the mouldy face?

The Flying Sauceress draws her ray gun

Flying Sauceress (*to Dodger and Bodger*) Citizens of London. Stand still. Do not move a muscle.
Dodger Who on earth are you?
Flying Sauceress (*to Dodger and Bodger*) Citizens of London. Stand still. Do

The audience, it is hoped, will be shouting to them to keep moving

Still! (*To the audience*) Silence! You evil earthling creeps. (*To Dodger and Bodger*) Stand *still*. (*To the audience*) Quiet!

Furious and frustrated, the Flying Sauceress exits

Bodger Ooooh!
Dodger (*to the audience*) Were you trying to tell us something?

Dodger and Bodger play this section as it comes, either getting individuals to talk, or the audience en masse. The aim is—as economically as possible— to establish, via the audience, that the Flying Sauceress will fluence people if they stand still, and will take them back to her planet

Thanks very much. Right. Come on, Bodger. Let's have a quick snooze now, then make an early start.

They settle down on a bench. Dodger gets under the eiderdown as Bodger removes his own trousers. His shirt is thus revealed to be a long nightshirt, perhaps with "Sleep Tight" written on it

Bodger What a day, Dad! Special licence from the Prime Minister ...
Dodger Meeting Old Father Time. Seeing his magical almanac with all the secret formulas that can control time ... What a day.
Bodger 'Night, Dad.
Dodger 'Night, Bodger.

Bodger gets under the eiderdown the other side. Both pull up the eiderdown, and realize their feet are sticking out. They rectify this, then repeat the gag. Bodger then turns on to his side, pulling the eiderdown off Dodger, who reacts and pulls it back. They repeat this, then start a tug-of-war with the eiderdown, which splits down the middle. Each gets under his own section of the eiderdown, then both go to sleep. They snore in unison. Pause

The Flying Sauceress enters. She sees they are asleep, and therefore still, exults and advances, drawing her ray gun

*The audience scream a warning to the Buskers, who wake up. The Flying Sauceress, after trying to shut up the audience, retreats and hides in the caravan. The Buskers stand and, realizing the audience is trying to warn them, encourage them to shout out what and where the danger is. Having gathered it is the green person who was there before, they go to look where they think the audience is pointing—*BEHIND *the caravan. As they disappear from view, the Flying Sauceress emerges and creeps round the front of the caravan. As the Buskers reappear from behind, she slips round the back. They shake their heads—no-one there. They try again, going round the other way to behind the caravan. The Flying Sauceress echoes their move and reappears at the front, trying to hush the audience. The Buskers re-emerge, and the Flying Sauceress hides again. The Buskers mime that they think the audience is having them on. Confidently they give up the hunt, return to their "bed" and settle to sleep. The Flying Sauceress sees her chance and quickly "fires" the fluence ray gun on each of them in turn— the ray gun lights up as she fires. Dramatic chord. Dodger and Bodger react fluenced*

Flying Sauceress Success! At last. Now I have had an idea of genius. If earth-lings will not stay still enough to be fluenced, I must force them to. By stop-ping time. If time stops, earthlings will be locked in one frozen position. Ready for my ray gun. And how do I stop time? Didn't I hear these stupid Buskers mention that they know Old Father Time who has an almanac which contains all the secrets of time? Well, then, this almanac must be mine. And these two must get it ...

Song 6   THE FLYING SAUCERESS'S APPRENTICE'S
                                    ASSISTANT

> (*Singing*)   Come morning light
>   At the destined hour
>   Fight as you might
>   You'll be in my power
>   Till I set you free.
>   Now say after me
>
>   I, Dodger, am now
>   The Flying Sauceress's apprentice
>   And I, Bodger, am now
>   The Flying Sauceress's apprentice's assistant.

Dodger and Bodger, zombie-like, rise from their sleeping positions and sit up

Dodger   I, Dodger, am now
                             The Flying Sauceress's apprentice.

Bodger   And I, Bodger, am now
                             The Flying Saucer cissy, the dentist's little sister.

The Flying Sauceress is tempted to hit him, but stops herself and continues

Flying Sauceress When you awake
                             You will rise and pack
                             Make no mistake
                             Steal the almanac
                             Bring it back to me
                             Then I'll set you free.

Dodger   I, Dodger, am now
                             The Flying Sauceress's apprentice.

Dodger lies down sharply

Bodger   And I, Bodger, am now
                             The sighing naughty Izzy has bent his kid's transistor.

Flying Sauceress (*speaking*) What?

Bodger   The lying false addresses that's rented to a twister
                             The flying horse who hisses and senses fishy business.

The Flying Sauceress makes magic passes towards Bodger, who then, with an effort, gets it right

The Flying Sauceress's Apprentice's Assistant.

Bodger lies down sharply

At the end of the song the Flying Sauceress, laughing, exits

Dodger and Bodger settle back to sleep. Music, as the Lights change to suggest a time lapse. Dawn creeps up, with bird song, and perhaps the distant sound of Big Ben chiming seven o'clock. Dodger wakes up. He appears perfectly normal, apart from a rather glazed, pop-eyed look

Dodger (*blinking, then realizing where he is*) Bodger. Wake up. (*He shakes Bodger*) Bodger. Time to get started.

Bodger wakes with a start. He comes quickly to his senses, but he also has a glazed, pop-eyed look

Bodger How are we going to do it, Dad?
Dodger I've got it all worked out. Disguise.
Bodger Disguise? Fancy dress?
Dodger Of course! You will wear a dress.
Bodger A dress?
Dodger That's right.
Bodger I don't want to wear a dress. I'll look soppy.
Dodger Don't argue. Hey up, let's get a move on.

They get up

Bodger Where are we going?

They throw the sleeping gear into the caravan

Dodger Where do you think, you ninny? Big Ben.

Dramatic chord, then music

Dodger and Bodger exit, dragging the caravan

The Lights fade to a Black-out

SCENE 5

At the top of Big Ben

It is December 31st—New Year's Eve. The time on the clock-face is exactly the same as it was at the beginning of Scene 2, which took place yesterday

The same routine is played out as took place in Scene 2, to establish the beginning of a normal day—but at a faster pace. Music is heard as the scene changes, and continues as we hear a couple of snores. Old Father Time is asleep in his bed. Suddenly the alarm bell rings violently, the hammer hits Old Father Time on the head, then knocks him down a couple of times as he tries to get up. As before, he stops the alarm, sits up, rolls up his beard, swings out his legs, and gets up. He covers his knees with his nightdress, letting the beard unroll, then

*gets up and trips over it. Under his breath he mutters "Drat and double drat".
He goes to the calendar and crosses off the 30th December. Then he goes to
the kennel and calls "Watchdog, Watchdog". As before, Watchdog leapfrogs
out over Old Father Time, then makes a fuss of him. Then, forgetting to wind
up Watchdog, Old Father Time gives him his oil. Watchdog drinks, then points
to the clock-face to remind Old Father Time of the nine o'clock sync*

   Old Father Time exits to check the main cog

*Watchdog waits on guard. Pause. Then the secret knock is heard, followed by
a voice from the main entrance or trap-door*

Bodger (*off, imitating Mrs Sparkle*) A stitch in time saves eight-and-a-half.

*Watchdog reacts exactly as if he has heard the real Mrs Sparkle. In fact, it is
hoped the audience will be taken in for a while, and think it IS the real Mrs
Sparkle. Watchdog opens the door*

   Bodger enters, disguised as Mrs Sparkle, with mop and bucket

   Morning, dearie.

*Watchdog barks a greeting. Bodger begins cleaning the floor, humming to himself
and acting suspiciously—in fact looking for the almanac, spotting it on the console, and working his way towards it. Just as he is within reach of it, the secret
knock is heard, and another voice from the main entrance*

Mrs Sparkle (*off*) A stitch in time saves eight-and-a-half.

Watchdog looks confused. Bodger hears the real Mrs Sparkle and hurries up

Watchdog opens the door and the real Mrs Sparkle enters

At the same moment, Bodger manages to reach the almanac

Mrs Sparkle (*arriving*) Morning, dearie.

*Watchdog, uncertain which is the real Mrs Sparkle, forces Mrs Sparkle back,
leaving the door open. Bodger is waiting his chance. Watchdog growls*

   What's the matter, dearie? It's only me.

Watchdog looks from one to the other. Mrs Sparkle sees Bodger. She gasps

   What the ...? Lor luvaduck!

*Bodger suddenly grabs the almanac and tries to make a run for it. Watchdog
leaps to the defence and tries to corner him. Whichever way Bodger turns, Watchdog turns also. Mrs Sparkle stays on the other side, mop poised to ward off attack.
Suddenly Watchdog starts to run down, as established in Scene 2. He manages
to reach the main door in jerks, but finally comes to a complete halt. Seeing
this, Bodger tries to escape, but Mrs Sparkle is advancing, mop outstretched.
Bodger senses danger, puts down the almanac and picks up his own mop. The
two charladies then engage in a dramatic sword fight, using their mops. After
several sallies, they reach a sort of deadlock position to one side of the room.
At this point the secret knock is heard, and a voice*

Dodger (*imitating Sergeant Watchit*) A stitch in time saves eight-and-a-half.

The audience should be really taken in by this impersonation. Visually it should be easy because of the distinctive uniform, and the busby hiding much of the head

   Dodger enters through the open door

Dodger sees the forlorn sight of the run-down Watchdog, who makes a desperate effort, barks, and nods towards the two Mrs Sparkles. Dodger, still Sergeant Watchit to the audience, fixes his bayonet and advances on the duellists. They stop, seeing him. He looks from one to the other, confused, then pinpoints, with his bayonet, the real Mrs Sparkle, allowing Bodger to slide away to the other side, where the almanac is. Mrs Sparkle, and doubtless the audience, point out "Sergeant Watchit's" error. He turns to see Bodger pick up the almanac. Apparently realizing his mistake, Dodger advances on Bodger. He chases him once or twice round the room. Each time they pass Mrs Sparkle, Bodger has to avoid being tripped by the mop. Eventually Bodger appears to give up. (This is all part of the Dodger/Bodger plan.) Under the threat, he hands over the almanac to Dodger, who raises it in triumph. The audience, it is hoped, will react, thinking good has triumphed! Leaving a threatening Mrs Sparkle to keep guard over Bodger, Dodger starts to leave—with the almanac: but as he reaches the entrance the secret knock is heard, and another voice

Sergeant Watchit A stitch in time saves eight-and-a-half.

   The real Sergeant Watchit enters

Dodger reacts quickly and keeps out of his eye-line

   Morning, Watchdog. (*He notices something is wrong with Watchdog, and bends to look at him*)

Sergeant Watchit What's the matter, old chap?

Dramatic music. Dodger raises the almanac above his head, preparing to strike Sergeant Watchit with it. In so doing, he knocks his busby back off his head, thus making it quite clear to the audience who he is. Mrs Sparkle spots the imminent attack on Sergeant Watchit, leaves Bodger, and grabs the almanac from behind Dodger's head. Then she raises it above her own head, in order to hit Dodger with it. Bodger spots this, rushes over and grabs the almanac from behind Mrs Sparkle's head. He then raises it above his own head in order to strike Mrs Sparkle, but—

   At this moment Old Father Time returns from checking the main cog. He gets in the way of Bodger's overhead swing of the almanac and gets hit. He collapses with a cry

At about this moment Sergeant Watchit, unaware of the fact that he was nearly brained, realizes what is wrong with Watchdog, and winds him up—sound effect. Mrs Sparkle rushes to nurse Old Father Time. Dodger and Bodger (who still has the almanac) realize they should make a dash for it. They aim for the main entrance, just as Watchdog is full of renewed vigour. Watchdog leaps, barking, on to Bodger, who tries desperately to hold on to the almanac. Meanwhile Dodger, who has replaced his busby, turns to face Sergeant Watchit. The Sergeant sees him—for the first time. Dodger thinks quickly, and salutes vehemently. Sergeant Watchit, temporarily confused, salutes back. In that second or two, Dodger rushes to grab Sergeant Watchit's rifle, which he has put down to attend to Watchdog. Dodger trains the rifle on Sergeant Watchit, who raises his hands nervously. They freeze, while the fight between Watchdog and Bodger continues. Watchdog virtually removes Bodger's dress and tickles him—he laughs hysterically and drops the almanac. Watchdog picks it up and, growling ferociously, holds it behind his back. He moves backwards towards the clock-face, stalked by a nervous Bodger. At the same time, Dodger forces Sergeant Watchit backwards towards the clock-face. Suddenly we hear the noise of the flying saucer. Bodger and Dodger react. They still have not got the almanac. Sergeant Watchit and Watchdog are now right up against the clock-face, Watchdog still clutching the almanac behind him and growling

> *Suddenly the Flying Sauceress appears outside the clock-face. Looking in and viewing the situation, she stealthily enters the door or window in the clock-face and simply grabs the almanac from Watchdog who, of course, has not seen her. She escapes*

The flying-saucer noise is heard as it leaves. Mission successful, Dodger "covers" Bodger with the rifle

> *Bodger exits through the main door. Then Dodger himself leaves, taking the rifle with him and closing the door behind him*

The music ends. Immediately Sergeant Watchit takes out his busby telephone and dials. Throughout the following scene he is urgently sending out messages which are heard as a murmur under the other action. Watchdog rushes to the door and starts to pull it open

Old Father Time No, Watchdog, no. We have work to do! It's nearly nine o'clock. (*He stands up, with difficulty*)

Mrs Sparkle Careful, dearie, careful.

Sergeant Watchit (*on the phone*) Hallo, security? ... Watchit here. Emergency Alert. Green space lady has stolen Old Father Time's almanac. (*He continues talking under the following speeches*)

Watchdog and Mrs Sparkle help Old Father Time to the console. He and Watchdog put on their earphones. He turns a knob—electronic noises are heard and lights flash, as in Scene 2

Old Father Time Father Time calling. Father Time calling. Greenwich Mean Time, Independent Radio News and B.B.C. Due to unforeseen circumstances, I am late. Please all stand by. Nine o'clock synchronization. Big Ben—GO!

The chimes preceding the single clangs start

(*Half-way through the chimes*) Greenwich Mean Time. Stand by with pips. And—GO!

The six Greenwich pips start. On the sixth the first booming Big Ben starts, followed by eight more

(*During the strike*) I.R.N. and B.B.C. stand by for news bulletins. (*Just after the last clang*) GO!

Radio Voice 1 ⎱ Good morning and welcome to the latest news ⎰ *Speaking*
                   ⎰   from I.R.N., with the time at nine o'clock ... ⎱ *together*
Radio Voice 2 ⎰ It's nine o'clock. This is B.B.C. Radio Four.
                       And here is the news ...

Old Father Time clicks off a switch, turning off the I.R.N. voice. The B.B.C. voice continues

Radio Voice 2 The Unidentified Object over London. It is now thought to be a flying saucer. (*Pause, then a rustle of paper*) I'm sorry, I have just been handed an urgent news flash. A few minutes ago, Old Father Time's almanac, which contains all the secrets of time, was stolen from his office in Big Ben. First reports hint that the theft was carried out by a Green Flying Sauceress, who left her flying saucer and invaded Big Ben. Our spokesman says that in the wrong hands, Old Father Time's almanac could bring about world chaos.

Dramatic chord. All look at one another, concerned, as the Lights fade to a Black-out

SCENE 6

The composite Westminster set

To facilitate the scene change, the Lights could fade to the Black-out before the news broadcast, but this should be avoided if possible as it could destroy the atmosphere of the closing moments. Another possibility is a linking set of chimes. The present scene starts at about 11 a.m. A pin spot on the face of Big Ben in the composite set could point out the fact that the time has moved on a couple of hours: alternatively, the Big Ben part of the composite set can be placed in position first, and music then accompanies the revolving of the clock hands in a pin spot, changing from nine to eleven, during the rest of the set change

When the Lights come up in the street, a few Tourists are wandering about. Sergeant Watchit is marching up and down: his "beat" is between his sentry-box and an unseen mark off. He is just marching on. He looks concerned, his march is agitated. He reaches his sentry-box, does the correct about-turn, then marches back and exits

Surreptitiously, trying not to be noticed, the Prime Minister enters from the arched entrance. He looks in the sentry-box then realizes that Sergeant Watchit must be marching. He spots him off and goes to meet him. They confront each other just in sight, during the conversation, the Sergeant cannot stop marching, so the Prime Minister has to move with him, backwards if necessary

Prime Minister Watchit.

Sergeant Watchit (*quite loudly, though on the move*) Sir!

Prime Minister Sssh! I don't want people to notice me. They might think something funny's going on.

Sergeant Watchit If they observe you walking like that, sir, no-one could blame them. Looks as though you're dancing with me.

Prime Minister Oh. (*He turns and walks forward, just as the Sergeant does his about turn*) Now listen—(*he realizes he has lost the Sergeant and dashes back to catch him up*)—have you spotted anything, Watchit?

Sergeant Watchit No, sir, no sign of the almanac *or* the Flying Sauceress, I'm afraid.

Sergeant Watchit exits. The Prime Minister shrugs his shoulders and exits through the arched entrance. By this time all the Tourists also have left

The moment the Prime Minister disappears the noise of the flying saucer is heard. It stops

The Flying Sauceress enters stealthily on the rooftop. She carries the almanac

Flying Sauceress Now is my moment. I will stop time, and then ...

Suddenly Sergeant Watchit returns. The Flying Sauceress exits out of sight hurriedly. Sergeant Watchit reaches his sentry-box, about-turns and exits again. The moment his back is turned the Flying Sauceress returns and signals mysteriously below.

Dodger and Bodger enter zombie-like in response to her signal, but quickly, and in step with each other

The Flying Sauceress claps her hands. Dodger and Bodger stop and appear to wake up

Catch! (*She throws down the almanac*)

They catch it

Chant the formula, TO STOP TIME. (*She prepares her ray gun*)

Dodger and Bodger stand at the edge of the stage and prepare themselves

Bodger (*looking in the almanac*) Ooh. It's all in a funny language, Dad.

Dodger Quick, Bodger, chant it.

Bodger I hope it's the right formula. (*He gulps and takes a deep breath*)

Song 7   MIRABILE DICTU (formula)

Bodger (*having difficulty in pronouncing the Latin*)
                              Mirabile dictu orbe tum
                              Incitate accelerate nunc ipsum

As Bodger sings, various people enter the street. These are selected for the type of movement their jobs require, to add to the visual impact of the following section. Other people also may be used should the size of the cast permit. (1) A Window Cleaner—with ladder and bucket. (2) A Postman—coming to empty the post-box. (3) A Road Sweeper—with broom.

Also entering the street are Mrs Sparkle, coming from work and so emerging from the arched entrance; and Sergeant Watchit, returning to his sentry-box

At the end of the formula, a dramatic noise and music continues as all the action is speeded up. If possible a flicker-wheel may be used, in the fashion of a silent film. Even the Flying Sauceress is moving faster—but NOT Dodger and Bodger, because they are holding the almanac and are therefore, as controllers, immune. After enough time has passed to establish the idea, with everyone carrying out their activities fast, the noise decreases

Flying Sauceress No, no, no!

Bodger Dad, Dad, I think I did the wrong one, Dad. Everything's going faster, Dad!

Dodger Calm down, Bodger. What did Old Father Time say to ... Correct ... Correct ... Got it! (*He shouts, making sure he is holding the almanac*) Correct to norm.

Immediately all is back to normal, and in the street the activity continues at a normal pace. The Postman empties the box, the Window Cleaner moves his ladder to another window and climbs it, etc.

Flying Sauceress (*hissing from above*) You stupid busker, get it right.

Bodger But it's all a sort of code, I ...

Dodger (*turning the pages*) Try this one, quick.

Song 7 (*continued*)   MIRABILE DICTU (formula)

Bodger Mirabile dictu orbe tum
        Recedete et commutate nunc ipsum.

At the end of the formula the Postman, having finished, is going to exit; the Window Cleaner is up the ladder; the Road Sweeper has crossed the stage and is almost out of sight; Mrs Sparkle is having a conversation with Sergeant Watchit, accompanying him on his march—they may well be aware that something odd is happening, but at no point should they appeal to the audience for advice. At the end of the formula there is a dramatic noise, and music that continues as everything goes backwards. At normal speed, everyone does the reverse of what they have already done. The Postman walks backwards to the post-box, puts back the letters, etc.; the Window Cleaner comes down his ladder, walks backwards with it to its former position, etc.; the Road Sweeper sweeps backwards; Mrs Sparkle and Sergeant Watchit move backwards on his "beat". The backwards action continues until everybody has returned to his or her first position on entering the stage at the beginning of the first formula—but about halfway through the backwards sequence the music softens

Flying Sauceress (*moving backwards too*) What have you done now?

Dodger Oh, no, they're all going backwards!

Bodger Dad, I don't like this, it's spooky!

Dodger Pull yourself together. Quick, find another formula.

Bodger turns the pages of the almanac

  Correct to norm!

Immediately all is back to normal, and everyone in the street is at their first positions. They start their action again

    The Prime Minister enters, intent on speaking to Sergeant Watchit

Flying Sauceress (*hissing from above*) Bodger, Dodger, I'm losing my patience.

She emphasizes the last word rather loudly, and it is heard by the Prime Minister, who turns and sees her, and also Dodger and Bodger, who are frantically leafing through the almanac

Prime Minister Suffering Tories! Watchit! And don't say "Sir"! Quick, phone Father Time. And stop marching up and down like a robot. Tell him his almanac's here. Then arrest that green person.

Sergeant Watchit somehow manages to take it all in. He dials. Meanwhile Bodger and Dodger find another formula

Song 7 (*continued*)   MIRABILE DICTU (formula)

Bodger Mirabile dictu orbe tum ...

Sergeant Watchit shouts over the formula

Sergeant Watchit (*on the phone*) Almanac. Down here.

Sergeant Watchit advances towards the rooftop. The Prime Minister advances towards Bodger and Dodger, followed closely by Mrs Sparkle. The other people in the street realize something is up and watch, though still doing their jobs

Bodger Iterate, redintegrate nunc ipsum.

As soon as the formula has finished, everybody except Bodger and Dodger goes into an "in the groove" routine, helped by music which repeats a phrase. Every five seconds or so everyone "jumps" back to where they started, like a gramophone record sticking. This means that the Prime Minister has just reached Dodger and Bodger by the end of the formula, but is pulled back by it, then stuck in a groove going back and forth to them. Similarly, Mrs Sparkle and Sergeant Watchit, attacking the Flying Sauceress with Mrs Sparkle's mop. Just as it gets near her the formula jerks it back, then back and forth in the groove. It may help to have one verbal phrase also in the groove—e.g. the Prime Minister saying "Now look here ..."

Bodger (*after a few "grooves"*) Ooh, Dad, look!
Dodger (*looking*) The needle's stuck! They're all locked in the same groove. Come on, find another formula.
Bodger I've had enough, Dad. I don't want to play any more. (*He starts to cry*)

Dodger Oh, for goodness sake! (*He grabs the almanac and starts turning pages*)

Meanwhile the groove routine of everyone else continues

    Suddenly Old Father Time, carrying his sickle, and Watchdog appear at the arched entrance. They are immune to the "groove". Old Father Time takes in the scene. He rushes to the Buskers and touches the almanac

Old Father Time (*shouting*) Correct to norm!

Everything goes back to normal. People react to the fact that they were stuck doing the same thing. There is general bewilderment. Old Father Time grabs the almanac from a surprised Dodger and Bodger. It is still open

Flying Sauceress (*escaping from Sergeant Watchit*) Aaaaah! The almanac.

Dodger grabs it back from Old Father Time

Old Father Time Give it back this minute. You're meddling with things you don't understand.
Dodger Sorry, Father Time, we've got to do it. Bodger, try this one. (*He points to a formula*)
Bodger Oh Dad, must I? (*He points to a formula*)

Watchdog tugs at Dodger. Mrs Sparkle sees the struggle and comes to join in. There is almost a tug-of-war going on, with the almanac in the middle. All the others gather round to watch the action

Flying Sauceress Do it, Bodger, do it!

Song 7 (*continued*)   MIRABILE DICTU (formula)

Bodger Mirabile dictu orbe tum
              Avolate et commutate nunc ipsum

As Bodger starts chanting, Old Father Time shouts over

Old Father Time No, no, no. Not *that* formula. Please. You idiots. Stop! It's not a controlling formula—it's a travelling formula. I can't correct it—*stop!*

Too late. Bodger finishes the chant. Noise—musical and electronic. If possible, as the formula starts to work, a ticking sound. What happens is that those holding the almanac—i.e. Dodger, Bodger, Old Father Time, Mrs Sparkle and Watchdog, travel backwards through time. To gain this effect they all stay where they are, moving their bodies to suggest being buffeted by the impact

   Everyone else exits backwards

Big Ben's hands start revolving backwards. The composite set, in stages, disappears as we go back through the ages. Meanwhile, if possible the Lights change to a flicker-wheel to suggest the days and nights flying past. When finally the noise and pandemonium cease and everything comes to a standstill, the five characters and the almanac are in the same positions as they started in, but on a virtually bare stage—against, say, a cyclorama. There is just one largish rock. We are, in fact, in prehistoric London

Bodger (*his knees knocking with fright*) Oooooh.
Dodger Shut up, Bodger.
Bodger Has it finished?
Old Father Time Yes, we've stopped.

Bodger Good, good. (*He looks up*)
Old Father Time I wouldn't be so sure. I don't know *when* we've stopped.

Watchdog barks—a sort of howling bark

Mrs Sparkle It's all right, dearie. All over. Let's go home.

They turn to go

Up them apples and pears! (*She stops aghast. There is no arched entrance!*)
Oo-er! Where's everything gone, Father Time? (*To the Buskers*) What have
you two done?

All turn and see that the location appears to have changed

Bodger Oooooh.
Dodger Shut up, Bodger. Where are we, Father Time?
Old Father Time Considering you two got us here by stealing my almanac
and fooling with formulas you don't understand, I'm surprised you have
the nerve to ask. But if you must know, we are exactly where we were, but
many years, maybe centuries, in the past. Long before the Houses of Parliament were built. That formula was very strong. We could be facing all kinds
of horrific dangers ...

*A strange, menacing animal noise makes everyone jump. All look off and react
horrified and terrified—even Watchdog. (Optional: a frightening shadow looms
large against the rock) Mrs Sparkle screams*

Bodger D-d-d-d-dad.

Watchdog barks furiously

Dodger Saints preserve us, what is it?
Old Father Time Fascinating! We must have travelled back to Prehistoric
London. That looks to me like—a dinosaur!

All panic and dash for shelter behind the rock. Music builds

The Dinosaur enters. It is not enormous (*the shadow on the rock made it seem
large*), but it looks ugly and sinister as it sniffs hungrily about. (*The Dinosaur
has to become quite lovable in Act II, so the face should have pleasant possi-
bilities, but the body is scaly, with shell-like appendages*)

The Dinosaur picks up a scent and stomps behind the rock

Old Father Time and the others emerge terrified, and scatter off in all direc-
tions. Dodger and Bodger exit on opposite sides from each other

*Pause. The Dinosaur lumbers out from behind the rock. He carries, and looks
at with curiosity, the magic almanac. There is a dramatic drum-roll, and—*

the CURTAIN *falls*

ACT II

SCENE 1

Prehistoric London

The scene begins a short while after the end of the previous Act and the setting is unchanged—just the rock and cyclorama, suggesting a barren landscape

Tension music is heard as Bodger enters, walking backwards warily, from one side of the stage. He is keeping a look-out for the Dinosaur, and is also nervous because he is alone

Bodger Oooooh!

After a few seconds Dodger enters from the opposite side, behaving in the same way

The two Buskers cannot see each other because they are back to back. In panto-mime tradition they come parallel to each other, then start circling, still back to back. After turning full circle they slowly walk backwards towards each other. They bump, scream and jump violently, then see each other

Dodger Bodger! Thank goodness it's you. But don't creep up on me like that!
Bodger I didn't, Dad. You crept up on me!
Dodger I didn't.
Bodger You did.
Dodger Didn't.
Bodger Did.
Dodger Didn't.
Bodger Did.

They are almost coming to blows when we hear the noise of the flying saucer. They hear it too, and freeze, zombie-like and frightened

The Flying Sauceress enters. She sees them

Flying Sauceress There you are. Thought you'd escaped my clutches, did you?
Dodger No ...
Flying Sauceress Had you thought a little harder you would have grasped that such a scheme was futile. I, too, can travel through time—on my saucer.
Bodger I chanted the wrong formula. They're all in a funny language.
Flying Sauceress Well. Now you will chant the *correct* formula and return to work. Open the almanac.

Pause. The Buskers shuffle nervously

I said open the almanac.

Dodger We can't.
Flying Sauceress Why not?
Bodger We've lost it.
Flying Sauceress (*shouting*) Lost it?
Bodger W-w-w-w-well—not exactly lost it. We just—can't find it. There was
this dinosaur—
Dodger —all scaly and ugly and horrible ...

They demonstrate, giving their dinosaur impersonations

Flying Sauceress (*moving between them*) A dinosaur! You fools. You lost the
almanac, then you invent this cock-and-bull story ...
Bodger It wasn't a cock ...
Dodger And it wasn't a bull ...
Bodger }
Dodger } It was a dinosaur.   { *Speaking*
                                                                       { *together*

Music

> *The Dinosaur enters, perhaps from behind the rock, stealthily, carrying the
> almanac*

Flying Sauceress Ridiculous.
Bodger It wasn't ridiculous. It was an elongated, monstrous beast, with a
revolting face and a spiky tail
Flying Sauceress Nonsense. Such a creature does not exist.

*By this time the audience should be shouting out that the Dinosaur is there. They
will not do this out of any desire to protect the Flying Sauceress, but (a) they
will want Bodger and Dodger—even though they are baddies now they are unwit-
ting baddies—to be proved right, and (b) they will want to see the Flying Sauceress's reaction to the beast. The Flying Sauceress shakes her head in disbelief,
looking at Bodger. If necessary a little argumentative dialogue may be ad-libbed.
Meanwhile the Dinosaur approaches Dodger, unseen by the others. Its paw
tickles him on the leg. He brushes his leg as though getting rid of a fly which
has landed there. This is repeated a couple of times—on Dodger's arm, then
his ear. This time Dodger catches the paw. Puzzled, he feels it for a second or
two. Then his expression turns to one of horror as he looks to the audience for
confirmation of what he fears*

> *Finally Dodger turns his head, sees the Dinosaur, screams and exits*

*The Dinosaur slips behind the Flying Sauceress, over to Bodger, just as the Flying
Sauceress, hearing the scream, turns to see Dodger dashing off. She calls after
him angrily, thinking he has escaped, rather than that he has seen the Dinosaur.
As she stamps her foot and beckons him back, looking off, the Dinosaur edges
behind Bodger and the Flying Sauceress, and, without their seeing, manages to
tap them both on the shoulder, then retreat a little. Both react angrily, thinking
the other tapped the shoulder. They argue a moment, then the business is
repeated: the Flying Sauceress looks off after Dodger—shoulder taps—argu-
ment. Then the Dinosaur taps Bodger's other shoulder. He turns, sees the Dino-*

saur, nods a greeting, turns his head back to the audience, then does a "slow burn" reaction ending in a huge double-take

   Bodger screams and exits

Hearing the scream, the Flying Sauceress turns, to see Bodger disappearing. She is angry at his escape, but still cannot see the Dinosaur, who starts looming up behind her. She moves towards the spot where Bodger exited, stalked by the Dinosaur, who then puts down the almanac on the ground and retreats up-stage. She turns and trips over the almanac, falling headlong. She is cross. She looks for the cause of her trip, and sees the almanac

   The almanac! (*She moves to it, bends down to pick it up*)

Meantime, however, the Dinosaur rushes round and grabs, or stands on, the almanac. The Flying Sauceress comes face to face with the Dinosaur and reacts in horror and surprise, staying stock still for a moment, then backing away slowly, screaming, and hiding behind the rock. The Dinosaur suddenly picks up his trophy—the almanac—and happily, even jauntily, wanders off

   The Dinosaur exits

The Flying Sauceress emerges from hiding

   That ferocious four-pawed fiend has the almanac. Must get it back. Must get it back. But how? Think nasty thoughts. (*She closes her eyes for a few moments*)

Music

   (*Suddenly*) Got it! Oh, a vintage nasty thought! Ha, ha, ha.

The music continues. After concentrating hard, she makes magical passes, and cruelly beckons on what she has conjured up—a tribe of Cavemen, five in all, including a Head Caveman and a Cavewoman. They carry spears

Song 8	UG!

Music

Cavemen ⎫	Ug!	⎧ *Singing*
Cavewoman ⎭	(*Music*)	⎩ *together*
	Ug!	
	(*Music*)	
	Ug ug!	
	(*Music*)	
	Ug ug!	
	(*Music*)	

In the routine, one of the Cavemen goes wrong—moves in the wrong direction or bumps into the others

	Ugga ugga ugga ugga
	Ug ug
Wrong Caveman	Oh!

All	Ugga ugga ugga ugga
	Ug ug
Wrong Caveman	Ow!

The others prod him or stand on his foot

All, except ⎫	
Wrong Caveman ⎬	Ha ha ha ha ha ha ha
Wrong Caveman (*sobbing*)	
	Boo hoo hoo hoo hoo hoo hoo

The Cavemen huddle together. The Cavewoman comes forward, shivering

Cavewoman	Brrrrrr!
	Brrrrrr!

A Gallant Caveman approaches, and sees she is cold

Gallant Caveman	Ahhhhh!
	Ohhhhh!

He turns and starts to remove one of his skins. A second Gallant Caveman approaches

Cavewoman	Brrrrrr!
	Brrrrrr!
Gallant Caveman 2	Ohhhhhh!
	(*Having an idea*) Ahhhhhh!

He starts removing a skin, too

Cavewoman (*smiling in anticipation*)

Mmmmmmmmmm! Mmmmmmmmmmm!

Both Gallant Cavemen approach, holding out a skin to warm her. They see each other

Gallant Caveman 1	Mmm haa.
Gallant Caveman 2	Mmm haa.
Both Gallant Cavemen	Grrrrrr!
	Grrrrrr!

They prepare to fight

Cavewoman	Ahhhhhh!
	Eeeeeee!

There is a stylized fight, very balanced

Gallant Caveman 1	Grunt
Gallant Caveman 2	Grunt
Gallant Caveman 1	Grunt
Gallant Caveman 2	Grunt
Gallant Caveman 1	Grunt
Gallant Caveman 2	Grunt

They make frustrated noises—because neither is winning

Gallant Caveman 1	Grunt
Gallant Caveman 2	Grunt
Gallant Caveman 1	Grunt
Gallant Caveman 2	Grunt
Gallant Caveman 1	Grunt
Gallant Caveman 2	Grunt

They make the frustrated noise again

Both Gallant Cavemen (*as if to say "Well, we're equal! Congratulations"*)
        Hoooooooo!

They shake hands and move away

        Aaaaaaaaaaaaa!
        Ha ha ha ha

The Cavewoman is left alone—back at square one

Cavewoman   Brrrrrrrrr!

All start the dance again

All   Ugga ugga ugga ugga
        Ug ug
        (*Yawn*)
        Ugga ugga ugga ugga
        Ug ug
        (*Yawn*)

They appear tired

        Ugga ugga ugga ugga
        Ug ug
        (*Yawn*)

They continue, getting slower

        Ugga ugga ugga ugga
        Ug ug
        Zzzzzzzzzzzzzzz.

All, leaning on one another, appear to go to sleep. Suddenly they "wake up"

        (Suddenly) UG!

After the song, one of the Cavemen indicates his stomach and gives a grunt which tells his fellows that he is very hungry. The others give grunts and groans of agreement. The Head Caveman grunts authoritatively and bangs his spear. The others listen. The Head Caveman grunts an encouraging, defiant speech, in which, pointing to his spear, he declares it is essential to catch and kill something to eat. The others punctuate his "speech" with "Hear, hear" type Og, Og sounds and guttural cheers
One of the Cavemen pretends to be an animal. The others laugh as it mock-attacks them. In a mock fight they pretend to attack it. As this is going on, the

Flying Sauceress emerges unnoticed, makes more magical passes, and beckons on the Dinosaur, still clutching the almanac. When the Cavemen spot the Dinosaur they stop their game and become very serious. The Flying Sauceress retreats behind the rock, while the Head Caveman organizes the Cavemen. They slowly encircle the unsuspecting Dinosaur as it looks at the almanac. Then, holding their spears horizontally in front of them, they close round and encapture the Dinosaur, who notices, panics, and unsuccessfully tries to escape from the ring of armed Cavemen. Then they start walking round the Dinosaur, as though preparing for the kill, chanting

Cavemen (*thrusting their spears in the air*)   Grunt
   (*beating their chests*)   Ug
   (*rubbing their tummies*)   Yummy, yummy, yum
   (*thrusting their spears in the air*)   Ug

They conclude the chant with a war cry, a sort of Red Indian hand-and-mouth noise. Then they all turn on the spot and start again, going in the opposite direction. As the chant progresses the Dinosaur becomes rather dazed and glazed, but still clasps the almanac. The chant continues at a lower level of intensity

   Old Father Time, Watchdog and Mrs Sparkle enter. Watchdog spots the strange ritual, and barks

Mrs Sparkle What, dearie? Oo-er! (*She sees the Cavemen*) Father Time!
Old Father Time (*turning*) Hickory, dickory, Mrs Sparkle, do you see what I see?
Mrs Sparkle A whole lot of them wrestlers on the telly.
Old Father Time No, no, they must be prehistoric cavemen. But can't you see what they've got in the middle?
Mrs Sparkle Belly-buttons?
Old Father Time No, no—the Dinosaur! And what's it clutching?
Mrs Sparkle Lor luvaduck! The chimney-stack.
Old Father Time Chimney stack?
Mrs Sparkle Yes! It's holding the chimney-stack—(*encouraging the audience to join in*—ALMANAC!

Watchdog rushes forward to rescue the almanac

Old Father Time No, Watchdog, back! They're dangerous.
Mrs Sparkle Yes. They might fancy you for afters.

Watchdog comes back—very slowly. He is trying to say something. He barks

Old Father Time What is it? Do you want winding up?

Watchdog shakes his head and mimes more deliberately, moving in slow motion, waving his arms

Mrs Sparkle I reckon as 'ow he's trying to tell us something.
Old Father Time (*trying to interpret the mime*) You're going for a swim?

Watchdog shakes his head and does it again, pointing at the Cavemen

   Slow motion?

Watchdog barks "Yes"

  Who?

Watchdog indicates the Cavemen

  The Cavemen? What? Slow them down so we can rescue the almanac?

Watchdog barks "Yes"

  Well, it's a thought. But to make them move in slow motion, we'd have to be holding the almanac when we say the formula!

Mrs Sparkle (*after a pause*) I'll do it!

Old Father Time What? No, Mrs Sparkle, I couldn't possibly permit it. It's too risky.

Mrs Sparkle You watch! What's the formula?

Old Father Time Oh dear, I can't remember! But it's on page twenty-two.

Mrs Sparkle Right. Page twenty-two. Here goes. Wish me luck, duck.

Old Father Time Good luck, Mrs Sparkle. You're a brave woman.

Watchdog barks "Good luck"

  And don't forget to "Correct to norm"!

Mrs Sparkle leaves her bucket with Old Father Time, then tentatively approaches the circle of Cavemen, lifting her mop as if it were a spear. She joins the circle. The Cavemen do not notice, as they are in a trance-like state. She does a couple of circuits, joining in all the noises and movements. At first she does it a little nervously, but ends up really rather enjoying it. In the circle, the Dinosaur is in a hypnotized state, because of the chanting and movements. He still holds the almanac. Mrs Sparkle joins the Dinosaur in the centre. She carefully flips the pages of the almanac until she finds the relevant one; then, still moving in time with the Cavemen's chant, utters the formula

Song 8A   MIRABILE DICTU (formula) [*reprise*]

Mrs Sparkle (*having almost more trouble with the pronunciation than Bodger*)
                  Mirabile dictu orbe tum
                  Impellete tardate lente nunc ipsum.

Immediately everyone, except Mrs Sparkle and the Dinosaur, goes into slow motion. The Cavemen chant and move slowly, with low voices. Old Father Time and Watchdog, observing, slow down too. When the slow motion has established itself, Mrs Sparkle prods the Dinosaur with her mop and pushes it out of the circle towards Old Father Time and Watchdog, who react (slowly), but the Dinosaur is still in a hypnotic state and stays placid. At this moment the Flying Sauceress appears from behind the rock—moving very slowly

Flying Sauceress (*in a slow, deep voice like a tape-recorder going at the wrong speed*) What on Ufrenia—is going on?

Seeing the Dinosaur holding the almanac, she starts towards it, but Mrs Sparkle, moving at normal pace, intercepts and prods the Flying Sauceress with the mop, forcing her to enter the circle of Cavemen, where she has to stay, flailing her arms about—but still in slow motion. Mrs Sparkle rushes back and grabs the almanac from the Dinosaur

Mrs Sparkle Correct to norm!

Immediately the speed reverts to normal, and the Cavemen chant as they did before. The Flying Sauceress realizes she is in danger as the chant gets more violent and tries to break out, screaming. The Cavemen "wake" from their trance and, seeing their "catch" has changed, chase off after the Flying Sauceress. The audience will, it is hoped, cheer the temporary undoing of the villainess

　　The Cavemen and Flying Sauceress exit

During the above, Old Father Time, Mrs Sparkle and Watchdog shield the Dinosaur from the sight of the Cavemen

Old Father Time Oh, well done, Mrs Sparkle. A triumph!
Mrs Sparkle Yes. I thought it was pretty chunky myself!
Old Father Time And the almanac is safely back.

Watchdog barks protectively and takes possession of the almanac

　　All right, good boy. Take care of it.

Suddenly the Dinosaur awakens from his hypnotic trance, realizes what has happened, and leaps upon Mrs Sparkle

Mrs Sparkle Aaaah!

But she does not worry for long: the Dinosaur, with loud noises, is licking her face with gratitude for being saved

Old Father Time Oh, look, he's saying thank you. You saved his life.
Mrs Sparkle It's a very wet thank you! Get off! You daffy Dinosaur!
Old Father Time You know, I fancy he's not as dangerous as we suspected—
　　are you, Dinosaur?

The Dinosaur grunts

　　In fact, I think he's rather a young and affectionate Dinosaur. Aren't you?

The Dinosaur goes very coy and bashful, rubbing his face against, first, Mrs Sparkle, then Old Father Time

Mrs Sparkle Ah! You're rather sweet, aren't you, really?

She receives an extra sloppy kiss. Watchdog approaches and links paws with the Dinosaur, who gives him a hug

　　And Watchdog likes you too. Where's your mum and dad, eh?

The Dinosaur mimes that he has not got a mum and dad

Mrs Sparkle You haven't got a mummy or a daddy, Dinosaur? Oh dear. Are
　　you all on your own?

The Dinosaur nods sadly

Old Father Time I'm beginning to believe this is a suitable case for adoption,
Mrs Sparkle. Would you care to be taken care of by us, little Dinosaur?

The Dinosaur grunts

(*To the audience*) Shall we? Very well. What's your name?

The Dinosaur mimes that he has not got one

You haven't got one? You must have a name! Let's all try and think of
one for you. (*To the audience*) You as well. Any ideas? What shall we call
him?

*Audience participation. A name is selected from those suggested. For conveni-
ence, he will here be called "Derek"!*

Old Father Time (*eventually*) There you are, then! Derek the Dinosaur!

Song 9   PREHISTORIC PET

Old Father Time   I never saw
                                      A dinosaur
                                      Before
                                      And never was
                                      A dinosaur
                                      Mine before.

*Old Father Time and Mrs Sparkle sing together, with the odd contribution from
Watchdog*

Old Father Time ⎱He's not a giant brontosaurus   ⎰ *Singing*
Mrs Sparkle   ⎰He's not the monster minotaur   ⎱ *together*
                                   No, with one accord we chorus
                                   He's
                                   Derek
                                   The Dinosaur.

                                   Derek
                                   You needn't be lonely
                                   Derek
                                   It's lucky we met
                                   Derek
                                   The world's one and only
                                   Prehistoric pet.

                                   Derek
                                   You needn't be lonely
                                   Derek
                                   It's lucky we met
                                   Derek
                                   The world's one and only ...

Mrs Sparkle stops the song

Mrs Sparkle Sorry, dearie, but up here—(*pointing to her head*)—there is twink-
ling a very bright—cauliflower ear!

Old Father Time Cauliflower ear?

Mrs Sparkle Cauliflower ear—*(encouraging the audience to join in)*—IDEA! If *everyone* could shout out "Derek"— *(to the audience)*—could you?— whenever we come to it in the song, it'll just prove to him he'll be very happy with us and our friends.

Old Father Time Oh yes—excellent. Why don't you raise your mop as a signal every time we all have to sing "Derek"?

Mrs Sparkle Right; quick practice. Mop up—"Derek". Right? *(She tries it once or twice)* That's real chunky!

Song 9 *(continued)*   PREHISTORIC PET

Audience	Derek
Old Father Time **Mrs Sparkle**	You needn't be lonely
Audience	Derek
Old Father Time **Mrs Sparkle**	It's lucky we met
Audience	Derek
Old Father Time **Mrs Sparkle**	The world's one and only Prehistoric pet.
Mrs Sparkle	Now that we've found
Audience	Derek
Mrs Sparkle	The Dinosaur I am really rather chuffed 'Cos it's unusual to see 'em Well, except in a museum Where they're either skeletons or stuffed.
Audience	Derek
Old Father Time **Mrs Sparkle**	You needn't be lonely
Audience	Derek
Old Father Time **Mrs Sparkle**	It's lucky we met
Audience	Derek
Old Father Time **Mrs Sparkle**	The world's one and only Prehistoric pet.
Old Father Time	You'll be famous
Audience	Derek
Old Father Time	The Dinosaur True phenomenon unique For though you're young it's element'ry If you're in the twentieth cent'ry You're a real live animal antique.
Audience	Derek
All	You needn't be lonely

Audience	Derek
All	It's lucky we met
Audience	Derek
All	The world's one and only
	Prehistoric
	Definitely not phantasmagoric
	Prehistoric pet.
	You bet—
	The prehistoric pet.

At the end of the song, still holding the almanac, Watchdog barks a warning and points to his watch/clock, and makes "time to go" movements

Old Father Time Quite right, Watchdog, it would be dangerous to prolong our prehistoric visit.

Mrs Sparkle Yes. There might be the odd pterodactoceroceros or bronto-ballyborus just around the Little Jack Horner.

Watchdog and the Dinosaur bark or grunt to the rhythm "Little Jack Horner"

Mrs Sparkle Easy one. "Little Jack Horner"—*(encouraging the audience to join in)*—CORNER.

Old Father Time Gather round, then, everybody. Almanac, please, Watchdog. Thank you. (*He opens the almanac*)

All stand nearby

Mrs Sparkle Back to the present, dearie?

Old Father Time Well, I sincerely hope so, Mrs Sparkle. In time for my change-over at midnight. But it's a tricky formula—accuracy only guaranteed within a few hundred years! Hold tight, everybody.

Watchdog helps the Dinosaur. All touch the almanac

Song 9A   MIRABILE DICTU (formula) [*reprise*]

Old Father Time Mirabile dictu orbe tum
                    Recurrete restituete nunc ipsum.

Just before the formula ends, The Flying Sauceress enters, breathless, on one side of the stage, Dodger and Bodger on the other. Very quickly, they see one another, and also see what is happening

Flying Sauceress Quick, you busking buffoons. To the saucer!

The three hurry out

Noise starts—musical and electronic, and if possible the ticking. Logically it is the reverse of the sequence at the end of Act I, though dramatically the noise must build. Lighting again changes, if possible, to a flicker-wheel to suggest days and nights passing quickly, but after an initial blast-off feeling, reacted to by the four travellers, it levels out into a calmer atmosphere, and the lighting changes: alternatively a strange colour in a single spot could be used

Mrs Sparkle (*as the music and electronic noise calms*) You've done it, dearie! We're moving! It was a bit of the old touch and go for a moment.

Old Father Time Exactly, Mrs Sparkle. (*Indicating his hands on the almanac*) Touch and go!

Mrs Sparkle (*laughing*) Steaming ahead!

Old Father Time We're certainly travelling, Mrs Sparkle, but we're not moving.

Mrs Sparkle Eh? You can't travel if you stay where you are!

Old Father Time But that's the whole point. We're not travelling through place, or even space. We're travelling through the Fourth Dimension.

Mrs Sparkle The Fourth Dimension? What's that?

Old Father Time Time! (*He sings*)

Song 10   THROUGH THE FOURTH DIMENSION

(*Optional. During this song, or during a musical bridge within it, it would be possible to stage a magical ultra-violet light section, during which the travellers through time pass various objects. Although, strictly and logically speaking, they are in the same place, but travelling through time, dramatic licence suggests it would be effective to have, for instance, clouds or stars or stylized funny interpretations of the Milky Way or the Great Bear. However, directors and designers may have other ideas for passing objects—for instance objects to suggest passing periods of history—or simply an assortment of time objects—clock-faces, hourglasses, etc. It is emphasized that this is optional and not necessary to the plot: but it could provide a fascinating visual treat in a large-scale production*)

> Through the Fourth Dimension
> Diurnal suspension
> Our journey through time has begun
> What a thrill, what a myst'ry
> To travel through hist'ry
> Until we come back to square one.

Mrs Sparkle   Look, Julius Caesar is crossing the Thames
                      There's Boadicea about to invade
Old Father Time   See William the Conqueror crowned at Westminster
Mrs Sparkle   And Richard the Lionheart commence his Crusade.

They sing together, with Watchdog and the Dinosaur if desired

Both   Through the Fourth Dimension
                      Diurnal suspension
                      Our journey through time has begun
                      What a thrill, what a myst'ry
                      To travel through hist'ry
                      Until we come back to square one.

The Lights cross-fade to another area

The flying saucer enters, carrying the Flying Sauceress, Dodger and Bodger

Dodger (*speaking*) There they are, look! Through the mists of time.
Flying Sauceress Excellent. They're only sixty or seventy years ahead of us. A century at the most.
Bodger What are we going to do?
Flying Sauceress Catch up with them, of course!

Flying Sauceress	Through the Fourth Dimension	*Singing*
Dodger	Diurnal suspension	*together*
Bodger	Our journey through time has begun	
Dodger	What a thrill	
Bodger	What a myst'ry	
Dodger	To travel through hist'ry	*Singing*
Bodger	Until we come back to square one.	*together*

They "look" at history. The Flying Sauceress concentrates on steering

Dodger   Look there, Magna Carta is signed by King John
Bodger   There's Caxton inventing his printing machine
Both   King Henry the Eighth's getting married again and
                        Now see William Shakespeare is scribbling a scene.

Flying Sauceress   Through the Fourth Dimension
                        Diurnal suspension
                        My journey through time I begin
                        When I've chased them and raced them
                        And finally faced them

She produces her ray gun

                        My fluence will fight them and win.

The Lights now pick up both sets of travellers. The flying saucer gains a little ground. During the following section the two groups become aware of each other

Flying Sauceress   There's only a couple of decades between us
Mrs Sparkle   Look out, the saucer is catching up fast
Dodger
Bodger   }   Sauceress, hurry, the others have seen us
Old Father Time (*concentrating hard, holding the almanac*)
                        Almanac, quicken our pace through the past.

The noise increases. The flying saucer appears to fall behind

Flying Sauceress		*Singing*
Dodger	Ahh! They're forging out front!	*together*
Bodger		

Old Father Time	Ha ha! They're out of the hunt!	*Singing*
Mrs Sparkle		*together*

The flying saucer exits, its occupants waving furiously

Old Father Time	Through the Fourth Dimension	*Singing*
Mrs Sparkle	Diurnal suspension	*together*
	Our journey through time has begun	

What a thrill, what a myst'ry
To travel through hist'ry
Until we come back—
We're on the right track—
Until we come back
With the almanac—
Until we come back to square one.

Towards the end of the song, the composite Westminster set starts returning, as though at certain points in the journey through time we reach the moments when those buildings were built. Obviously, this is done in reverse order from the order in which the buildings disappeared at the end of Act I

SCENE 2

London. The composite Westminster set, but without Big Ben, sentry-box, railings, etc. The year is, in fact, 1605

The noise stops, the Lights return to normal. Old Father Time, Mrs Sparkle, Watchdog and the Dinosaur look gingerly round but, as yet, do not see that Big Ben is missing

Mrs Sparkle Real chunky, dearie! You've done it.

Watchdog barks. The Dinosaur grunts

Old Father Time Oh thank goodness, the Houses of Parliament! We're home. Now, let's see. Are we in time for my farewell party?
Mrs Sparkle I reckon as how we must be, 'cos otherwise *you* wouldn't be here!
Old Father Time True. So what *is* the time?

All turn to look at Big Ben. After a stunned pause Watchdog barks, mystified

Mrs Sparkle Oo-er! Big Ben's shrunk.
Old Father Time But it can't have.
Mrs Sparkle Well, dearie, it's either shrunk or sunk. Whatever way you look at it, it's gawn!
Old Father Time Unless—it hasn't been built yet.
Mrs Sparkle Eh?

Suddenly a loud noise from the door to the cellars (the trap-door if possible— the same one as that used in the "Top of Big Ben" scene). Watchdog barks furiously and sniffs around the door. Tension music, as the door opens. All retreat

A Beefeater enters. He carries a lantern and a sort of spear. He stands formally

Beefeater Nine of the clock and in the cellars all is well. (*He starts walking towards the arched entrance and prepares to open the door with a key on a large key-ring*)

Mrs Sparkle (*whispering*) What's a carpet-beater doing here?
Old Father Time (*whispering*) Carpet-beater?
Mrs Sparkle Yes. Carpet-beater—(*encouraging the audience to join in, whispering*)—Beefeater!
Old Father Time I don't know. Let's ask.

Old Father Time and Mrs Sparkle approach the Beefeater. Meanwhile Watchdog and the Dinosaur stand in the shadows, as it were, out of view of the Beefeater. They watch

(*To the Beefeater*) I say, excuse me ...

The Beefeater turns and stiffly points the spear at them, holding up his lantern

Beefeater Who goes there? Friend or foe?
Old Father Time Friend.
Mrs Sparkle Ditto. No foes here, dearie.
Beefeater I know you not, old man. Kindly come with me for the questioning. Thou also, ma'am.
Old Father Time But all I wanted to ask ...

The Beefeater threateningly forces them to move off

Mrs Sparkle That thing looks lethal. Just watch where you prod.
Old Father Time But where are you taking us?
Beefeater To the Head of the Yeomen of the Guard. All suspicious characters must be interrogated by him. (*He stops dramatically and looks closely at them*) In case you're one of the plotters.
Old Father Time What plotters?
Beefeater The plotters what are plotting to blow up the Houses of Parliament. Forward. (*He forces them on*)

They are about to exit off stage, not through the arched entrance

Old Father Time Excuse me, but what year is this?
Beefeater What?
Old Father Time What is the date?
Beefeater November the fifth.

Beefeater, Old Father Time and Mrs Sparkle exit

Watchdog and the Dinosaur emerge from hiding, concerned. Watchdog still holds the almanac. They exchange a bark and grunt of "What shall we do now?" but shrug their "shoulders" in helplessness. Suddenly we hear the flying-saucer noise: so do they, and react in fright. They bark and grunt as they decide to hide. Watchdog runs to the arched entrance, but it is locked. The Dinosaur points to the cellar door through which the Beefeater came. Together they heave open the door. (If it is a trap-door they help the tension by having to struggle.) Then the Dinosaur keeps watch for Watchdog. In a moment the saucer noise stops

Watchdog goes in, leaving the almanac on the ground. (If the door used is not a trap-door, Watchdog puts the almanac down in order to get a good pull on the door)

As soon as Watchdog disappears, the Flying Sauceress enters

The Dinosaur keeps watch, but looks in the wrong direction so that he cannot see the Flying Sauceress. He is some distance from the almanac

Flying Sauceress (*suddenly spotting the almanac, without seeing the Dinosaur*) The almanac! (*She goes to pounce on it*)

The Dinosaur, helped probably by a warning from the audience, leaps to the defence. Both freeze in mutual terror when they see each other, standing on either side of the almanac. There is a moment of frozen stalemate

> *Watchdog pops his head out of the cellar door, registers what has happened, grabs the almanac, barks an instruction to the Dinosaur, pointing off in the direction Old Father Time and the others went out, and pops back through the cellar door.*
> *The Dinosaur understands, makes a threatening growl, shakes his scales, then lumbers off to fetch help*

The Flying Sauceress lets him go, has an idea, tiptoes to the cellar door and closes it. (If it is a trap-door she stands on it; if not, she leans against it)

> Now the almanac is within my grasp. I *shall* stop time. I *shall* fluence. (*She produces her ray gun*) I *shall* find workers for Ufrenia. (*To the audience*) And *you* will be the first I fluence, if you give me away again. Do you understand? Now. Think nasty thoughts. (*She closes her eyes*)

Music

> (*Suddenly*) Got it! A classic nasty thought. Ha, ha, ha.

The music continues as, after concentrating hard, she makes magical passes and cruelly beckons on what she has conjured up

> *Five cloaked and hatted figures enter, two of whom are Dodger and Bodger. They are led by Guy Fawkes. Carrying lanterns, they enter in cloak-and-dagger style, holding their cloaks up over their faces. Once assembled, all except Guy Fawkes lower their cloaks, revealing their evil visages*

The Flying Sauceress stands to one side, in view, but not of the Conspirators. They, all except Guy Fawkes, whisper to one another in a buzz of "plotting rhubarb", simply repeating the word "Plot" to one another. After a while, Guy Fawkes dramatically lowers his cloak. The others notice this and pass the message on, in whispers

Conspirators Master Fawkes, Master Fawkes. (*They all do an exaggerated bow*)
Guy Fawkes Gentlemen.
Conspirators Good Master Fawkes.
Guy Fawkes This night is *the* night.
Conspirators (*in an awful "plotting rhubarb" echo*) Ay, this night is *the* night, 'tis true, ay ... etc.
Guy Fawkes Our labours have not been in vain.

Conspirators (*as before*) 'Tis true, no vain labours, he speaks the truth in troth, ay ... etc.

Guy Fawkes (*stretching out his fist*) Gentlemen.

They all cluster round, clutching fists as though sealing a pact

Down with the King.

Conspirators Down with the King.

Guy Fawkes Up with the Houses of Parliament.

Conspirators Up with the Houses of Parliament.

Guy Fawkes Up—sky high!

Laughter

Song 11   MUMBLE, MUTTER, MURMUR

The Conspirators stand in a plotting huddle

Conspirators Mumble, mutter, murmur
Nudge nudge, wink wink, hush hush
Psst psst, buzz buzz, shhhh!

Guy Fawkes Gents, commence assault!

Conspirators Stealthy, slinky, shifty
Sniff sniff, snoop snoop, sneak sneak
Creepy, crawly, shhhh!

Guy Fawkes Open up the vault!

During the next verse, the door to the cellars is opened, and one Conspirator descends, remaining with his head still in view

All   We're cloaked in strictest secrecy
Each Conspirator a brother
So secret no-one knows us
So secret we don't even know each other
There are those would sorely hate us
Call us traitors
In league
As we weave our web of vicious
And malicious
Intrigue.

Mumble, mutter, murmur
Nudge nudge, wink wink, hush hush
Psst psst, buzz buzz, shhhh!

Guy Fawkes Powder barrels roll!

The Conspirators begin rolling in barrels of powder towards the door

Conspirators Stealthy, slinky, shifty
Sniff sniff, snoop snoop, sneak sneak
Creepy, crawly, shhhh!

Guy Fawkes Heave 'em through the hole!

They do so. Then they prepare the fuse, which leads from the cellar across the stage to one side

All   We disapprove of Parliament
       So we vow to burst its bubble
       Right now you see it standing
       But in a while you'll see a pile of rubble.
       The explosion will be louder
       The more powder
       We use
       Now our desp'rate plot is hatching
       We're attaching
       The fuse.

       Mumble, mutter, murmur
       Nudge nudge, wink wink, hush hush
       Psst psst, buzz buzz, shhhh!

Guy Fawkes Stand by for the blast!

The Conspirators cluster round

Conspirators Stealthy, slinky, shifty
       Sniff sniff, snoop snoop, sneak sneak
       Creepy, crawly, shhhh!

Guy Fawkes Light the fuse—and fast!

A candle is removed from a lantern and raised. The action freezes as the Flying Sauceress comes forward. Tension music, drum roll

Flying Sauceress (*shouting towards the door to the cellars*) Watchdog! You have but seconds in which to come out—with the almanac—or be blown up with the Houses of Parliament.

Pause. Nothing happens

 Watchdog. Guy Fawkes is about to light the fuse. Come out!

Pause. Nothing

Bodger (*as one of the Conspirators, revealing for the first time who he is*) Pssst. (*He comes forward from the huddle*) Perhaps he's run down.
Flying Sauceress What?
Dodger (*joining Bodger*) Run down. He's clockwork. We saw him do it this morning.
Flying Sauceress Run down, eh? Very well. Bodger—"run down" and find out. (*She points to the cellar door*)
Bodger Oh no, please, I . . .

The Flying Sauceress raises her hand and Bodger becomes zombie-like

 Bodger exits through the cellar door

Pause. A muffled noise—a scream and a thud. Silence

Flying Sauceress (*worried, though trying not to show it*) Dodger, the cellars.

Dodger But ...

Too late—the Flying Sauceress raises her hand. Dodger becomes zombie-like

   Dodger exits through the cellar door reluctantly, but knowing he has no power to refuse

Pause. Another muffled noise—a scream and a thud. Silence

Guy Fawkes Light the fuse!

The Conspirators' action unfreezes. The fuse is held up in readiness

Flying Sauceress (*panicking*) The almanac ... (*To Guy Fawkes*) No, wait.
Guy Fawkes Wait? We have waited years for this moment. We will wait no longer.

The fuse is lit. With the use of a pin spot, and accompanied by tension music, the lit fuse creeps towards the cellar door

Flying Sauceress (*losing her usual coolness*) You stupid little earthling dog! Come out! Bodger! Dodger! You useless buskers! Guy Fawkes, stop it, stop it.

   In the nick of time the Dinosaur enters, leading the way for the Beefeater and the Head of the Yeomen of the Guard

The Dinosaur points at the scene. The Beefeater sums up the situation very quickly, and he and the Head of the Yeoman of the Guard rush in and round up the three remaining Conspirators

   The Flying Sauceress sees her chance and slips out unnoticed

Head of the Yeomen of the Guard Master Fawkes. I arrest you and your fellow conspirators in the name of the King. You will ...

He is interrupted by the Dinosaur grunting and pointing to the cellar door and the fuse which, still alight, is creeping towards it

   At this moment a breathless Old Father Time enters, followed closely by Mrs Sparkle

The audience will probably be shouting a warning about the fuse. They see it. Old Father Time rushes over and cuts it with his sickle. Mrs Sparkle follows and douses the "flame" with water from her bucket. Then she holds her hands above her head in a victory pose

Old Father Time What teamwork, Mrs Sparkle! (*Suddenly worried*) Watchdog! Where is he? (*Calling*) Watchdog!

The audience, and the Dinosaur, tell him where Watchdog is. He goes to the cellar door and opens it

   From it come Dodger and Bodger, with barrels over their heads. They stagger off, pushed by the others. Then there is a fanfare as Watchdog emerges proudly, with the almanac held high

Everybody, except the Conspirators, cheers. The Head of the Yeomen of the Guard walks forward

Head of the Yeomen of the Guard Mr Watchdog, in the name of the King, I thank you for your courageous behaviour. Indeed, I commend you all.

Beefeater Thanks to you, the Houses of Parliament stand firm and the King lives.

Guy Fawkes Creeps!

Head of the Yeomen of the Guard Silence, Master Fawkes!

Old Father Time Well done, Watchdog.

All cheer, and Watchdog, barking with pleasure, starts to join the others, but suddenly starts to run down. He comes to a complete stop

Head of the Yeomen of the Guard Is he ill?

Mrs Sparkle No dearie, just a little run down.

The Dinosaur rushes forward and winds up Watchdog—with all the sound effects. Watchdog perks up again

Head of the Yeomen of the Guard Splendid. Now, would you all care to be presented to His Majesty?

Mrs Sparkle (*excitedly*) Ooooooh!

Old Father Time (*hastily*) Thank you, but we must get back to nineteen seventy-six. My change-over ceremony must be any minute. (*He takes the almanac*)

Mrs Sparkle Yes, and I've left some sausage rolls in the oven.

The four travellers cluster round the almanac

Head of the Yeomen of the Guard Very well. Good luck!

Guy Fawkes
The Two Remaining Conspirators } Good riddance. } *Speaking together*

Mrs Sparkle At least we're going home, Guy Fawkes. You lot are going to be locked up in the shovel and pick.

Guy Fawkes
The Two Remaining Conspirators } Shovel and pick? } *Speaking together*

Mrs Sparkle Yes. Shovel and pick—(*encouraging the audience to join in*)—NICK!

Old Father Time Stand by! By the way, what year are *you* in, sir? I should remember from my history book, but ...

Head of the Yeomen of the Guard Sixteen-hundred and five.

Old Father Time Thank you. (*He does a few rapid mental calculations*) Farewell.

All say good-bye

Song 11A   MIRABILE DICTU (formula) [*reprise*]

Mirabile dictu orbe tum
Recurrete restituet nunc ipsum.

Noise and music as the formula starts working. The flicker-wheel starts up again if possible. The seventeenth-century characters, waving, move off

The Beefeater, Head of the Yeoman of the Guard, Guy Fawkes and Conspirators exit

Song 11B THROUGH THE FOURTH DIMENSION [*reprise*]

(Optional. Just as during Song 10, this could be an opportunity for imaginative "travelling through time" ultra-violet lighting effects)

Towards the end of the song, the composite set is made complete once more by the arrival of Big Ben and any other parts left off for the seventeenth-century section. A few seconds of noise and flicker-wheel complete the journey, during which Sergeant Watchit takes up his position at the sentry-box

Old Father Time	Through the Fourth Dimension
Mrs Sparkle	Diurnal suspension
Watchdog (*if desired*)	Our journey once more has begun
Dinosaur (*if desired*)	What a thrill, what a myst'ry
	To travel through hist'ry
	Until we come back to square one.

{ Singing together }

Look, there's the Great Fire and London's in flames
But see it rebuilt by Sir Christopher Wren

With mounting excitement

Just look at St Paul's and there's Westminster Abbey
And Buckingham Palace, and look, there's Big Ben!

Through the Fourth Dimension
Diurnal suspension

Old Father Time Our journey is practic'lly done
Mrs Sparkle What a thrill
What a myst'ry

Both We've travelled through hist'ry
All And now we've come back
The end of the track
Yes, now we've come back
With the almanac
And now we've come back to square one.

SCENE 3

The same. The Lights return to normal. It is late evening

The travellers are semi-frozen, their eyes closed. They gingerly look around

Sergeant Watchit Hallo, hallo, hallo!

They whisk round. Watchdog runs to the Sergeant

Mrs Sparkle (*relieved*) Oh, it's the Sergeant! Wotcher, Watchit, me old cocker spaniel!

Sergeant Watchit (*making a fuss of Watchdog*) Welcome home. What a pleasurable moment this is.

Old Father Time Thank you, Sergeant Watchit.

Sergeant Watchit Jeepers creepers: (*Indicating the Dinosaur*) What's that?

Old Father Time Allow me to introduce Derek the Dinosaur.

Sergeant Watchit (*nervously*) Pleased to make your acquaintance, I'm sure. (*To Old Father Time*) Is he house-trained?

Old Father Time Of course.

Sergeant Watchit holds out his hand, looking the other way in fright. The Dinosaur shakes it very courteously and grunts a polite greeting

Sergeant Watchit And the same to you—with knobs on.

The Dinosaur reacts hurt—looking at his appendages

Oh, I beg your pardon.

Mrs Sparkle Hey, I bet nobody's missed us.

Sergeant Watchit Believe me, Mrs S., deep concern was expressed at your disappearance, not least in the vicinity of my sentry-box.

Watchdog barks and points up to Big Ben, which says eleven forty-five

Old Father Time Quite right, Watchdog. I was forgetting. We're just in time for the change-over ceremony. Come on.

Sergeant Watchit Allow me to escort you (*loudly*)—SIR!

All jump, then run to the arched entrance. The Dinosaur is left behind

Mrs Sparkle Come on, Derek, up the apples and pears!

All exit, as the Lights fade to a Black-out

SCENE 4

The Other Part of London. Front cloth—darkness

After a second's pause the noise of the flying saucer is heard—it approaches and stops. The Lights come up

The Flying Sauceress enters, pushing on the Buskers, who still have the barrels over their heads

Flying Sauceress Why I ever lumbered myself with two such bungling buskers, I fail to think. You chant the wrong formulas, you lose the almanac, you're rendered helpless by a harmless earthling dog. What have you to say for yourselves?

Dodger and Bodger make muffled noises from inside the barrels

Flying Sauceress And take those stupid barrels off.

They do so

Do you realize, if I hadn't rescued you, at this moment you'd be locked in the Tower in sixteen hundred and five for taking part in the Gunpowder Plot?

Bodger Well, we haven't got used to being Sorceress's Apprenticesiziziz.

Flying Sauceress And you never will. I've suffered enough. I'm relieving you of all duties. From tonight, I work alone. I *shall* stop time. I *shall* fluence. (*To the audience*) Even if it means waiting until you earthlings are all in bed, asleep, still enough for the fluence to work! (*To the Buskers*) Come here, you two. (*She places her hands on their heads and chants*) "You fools have wasted my every hour. So I release you from my power." Now for the almanac.

The Flying Sauceress exits resolutely, leaving the Buskers trancelike

The flying saucer is heard taking off. The noise lessens as Dodger and Bodger "wake up"

Bodger (*in a slightly far-away voice*) Dad. Dad.

Dodger (*similarly*) Yes, Bodger.

Bodger My feet ache.

Dodger (*snapping out of it*) Stop rabbiting on about your ... (*Suddenly realizing*) Hey, Bodger, I've just had a horrible dream, a nightmare.

Bodger (*coming to*) So have I, Dad; it was dark and eerie and terrifying.

Dodger Why?

Bodger I had a barrel on my head!

Dodger Green—green face—almanac ...

Bodger Flying saucer—dinosaur ...

Dodger Guy Fawkes ...

Bodger Dad.

Dodger Yes, Bodger?

Bodger It wasn't a nightmare—it was *real*! (*He jumps into Dodger's arms, trembling with fear*)

Dodger You're right. Stopping time. The green face. Tonight.

Bodger We must do something to help. Warn Old Father Time.

Dodger Where is he?

The audience should shout out that he is back at the top of Big Ben

Bodger Of course, Big Ben.

Dodger Come on, Bodger. Quick.

Dodger and Bodger exit towards Big Ben, as the Lights fade to a Black-out

SCENE 5

At the top of Big Ben

Old Father Time's office has been decorated with flags, bunting, etc., in order to celebrate the change-over ceremony. A tray of drinks is being handed out by Watchdog and the Dinosaur. There are plates of party food. The huge hands of the clock point to 11.50

The party has begun. Present are the Prime Minister, Old Father Time, Mrs Sparkle, Watchdog, the Dinosaur, Sergeant Watchit, and such dignitaries as the Lord Mayor of London and his wife. They all stand listening to a toast

Prime Minister (*taking in the audience as guests too*) Your Worships, my Lords, Ladies and Gentlemen ...

Watchdog barks, the Dinosaur grunts

And animals. It is my pleasurable duty, or, should I say, my dutiful pleasure, on behalf of us all, to propose a toast to our esteemed colleague and trusted friend who tonight leaves us, having concluded twelve months' dedicated service.

Mrs Sparkle bursts into tears

Mrs Sparkle Ooh, I'm sorry, I'm sorry. I'm going to miss you, dearie. I can't help it.

Sergeant Watchit hands her a handkerchief, with which she gratefully wipes her eyes

Prime Minister Soon we will welcome the new Father Time. But now, with ...

He is interrupted by Mrs Sparkle wringing out a considerable amount of water from the handkerchief into her bucket

(*Trying again*) With our grateful ...

He is interrupted by Mrs Sparkle loudly blowing her nose into her upturned mop

Mrs Sparkle Beg pardon.
Prime Minister With our grateful thanks. (*Lifting his glass*) Old Father Time.

All raise their glasses

All OLD FATHER TIME

There is a sudden urgent knocking at the door (or trap-door). All fall silent, surprised, except Watchdog, who barks furiously

Dodger (*off, breathlessly*) A stitch in time saves eight-and-a-half.

Sergeant Watchit opens the door a little

Sergeant Watchit Who's there?
Dodger (*off*) Dodger and Bodger.
Old Father Time Dodger and Bodger?
Mrs Sparkle What a nerve. All day long they've been helping that flying green-gage and ...

The following section is taken very fast by Dodger and Bodger, as a virtuoso duet. They are breathless because of their long climb

Dodger's head appears

Dodger Please. You've got to listen. She fluenced us. We were under her power. (*He enters fully*)

Bodger's head appears

Bodger But we bodged everything so she released us. We've come to warn you. (*He enters fully*)

Dodger The Flying Sauceress is on her way. She's going to steal the almanac—

Bodger —stop time—

Dodger —fluence people—

Bodger —and make them her slaves. Oooh, she's horrible!

Pause

Prime Minister Is this true?

Bodger Cross my heart, Busker's honour. (*To the audience*) Isn't it?

Audience Yes.

Old Father Time Did you say she wants to *stop* time?

Dodger Yes, sir. Her fluence won't work unless the subject is absolutely still. (*He demonstrates a frozen position*)

Mrs Sparkle Well, if she tries to come the old fluencing with me, she'll get this—(*her mop*)—right up her pea-shooter.

Bodger Pea-shooter?

Mrs Sparkle Yes, pea-shooter—(*encouraging the audience to join in*)—HOOTER!

Old Father Time What are we to do? The change-over is in five minutes. I can't leave the responsibility for this with the new Father Time.

Dodger Look, sir, I've got a plan. Would you trust me to put into operation?

Old Father Time I ... (*To the audience*) Should we trust Dodger?

Audience Yes.

Old Father Time Very well.

Prime Minister I agree too.

Dodger Thank you, sir. Now, supposing, when the Flying Sauceress comes here in a minute, we made her think she had really stopped time—everyone frozen still ...

Bodger She'd try to fluence everyone.

Dodger Right. But suppose if in the nick of time everybody *moved*, so she couldn't fluence them!

Bodger That'd make her mad! She'd be taken right off her guard.

Dodger Exactly. And when she's off her guard, we all overpower her and catch her.

Mrs Sparkle Yes, that's real chunky, BUT—how do we make her think as how she's stopped time in the first place?

Dodger Good point. She'll arrive and try to find the almanac, right? We pretend not to notice her. She finds the formula and chants it ...

Old Father Time But there *isn't* a formula to stop time.

Dodger We *invent* one. You, sir, write any old rubbish, call it a "stop-time" formula, and leave it in the almanac.

Old Father Time Hickory, dickory, that's brilliant! I'll do it now. (*He rushes to the console and writes*)

Dodger So, she chants the phoney formula and we all freeze. Still as statues.

Bodger (*indicating the audience*) All of us?

Dodger *All* of us. (*To the audience*) Are you with us?

Audience Yes.

Dodger Right. We're all frozen. She thinks she's stopped time …

Sergeant Watchit Pardon me, Mr Dodger. A flaw in the scheme. Will the green lady not notice that Big Ben is still ticking away?

Dodger is momentarily floored

Old Father Time (*returning from the console, the finished formula in his hand*) Easy! I'll stop the main cog.

Prime Minister Stop Big Ben? That's unheard of.

Old Father Time An emergency, Prime Minister.

Prime Minister Oh, very well.

Dodger Good. So, we're all frozen. The Flying Sauceress prepares to fluence us, she aims her ray gun. And, at that moment all of us—(*taking in the audience*)—move, wave our arms and legs …

Bodger And we could shout "Tick, tock, tick, tock", too.

Dodger Good idea. Then she'll panic and Sergeant Watchit will be able to arrest her.

Sergeant Watchit My pleasure, Mr Dodger.

Mrs Sparkle We'd better have a quick practice, dearie; otherwise I reckon I might be moving when I'm meant to be froze.

Dodger All right. First, the almanac—

Watchdog, barking, produces it. He and the Dinosaur open it

—put the phoney formula inside—

Old Father Time does so

—and leave it fairly visible—on your console, sir.

The Dinosaur takes the almanac and positions it

Now, the Flying Sauceress arrives—who wants to play the Flying Sauceress?

Watchdog barks and raises his paw

Right, Watchdog. In you come. We pretend not to notice.

Watchdog, from now on, does his Flying Sauceress impersonation. He "enters" from near the clock-face and starts sniffing around. The others mime the party going on

You're searching for the almanac. You find it! You look for the "stop-time" formula. You find it!

Watchdog follows all the actions

You chant the formula—

Watchdog growls in a sort of sing-song but ends with a definite stop—the signal to freeze

Dodger —and we all freeze.

All freeze, including the audience—encouraged if necessary by Dodger and Bodger

Bodger Hey! Idea. Why doesn't everyone stand up? Then she'd see them better—it'd be more convincing.
Dodger Yes! (*To the audience*) If you want to, stand up! And we'll have a practice freeze! After three: one, two, three, FREEZE. Very good. Hopefully the Flying Sauceress is taken in.

Watchdog acts pleased and triumphant

She draws her ray gun—

Watchdog mimes this

—and at the vital moment ...
Mrs Sparkle (*still frozen, speaking without moving her lips*) How do we recognize the "vital moment"?
Old Father Time Use my alarm clock, if you like.
Dodger Prime Minister, could you give us the signal?
Prime Minister I'll do my best. (*He goes to the alarm clock Old Father Time shows him which switch to press*)

Dodger So the ray gun is up—it's the vital moment—and—

The Prime Minister presses the switch and the alarm bell rings violently

(*Shouting*)—we all move—arms—legs—heads! And say "Tick, tock, tick, tock".

All, including the audience, do this. The situation is established for a few seconds, then Dodger continues

The Flying Sauceress is taken by surprise, she panics—

Watchdog impersonates this very funnily

and Sergeant Watchit arrests her. (*Sergeant Watchit comes foward and "arrests" Watchdog*)

Cheers

Well done, everybody!
Old Father Time When I hear the alarm, I'll turn the main cog back on, shall I, Dodger?
Dodger Yes, please, sir. Back to normal then!

Optional Section

Dodger Now, shall we try all that again, just to make sure we all know what we're doing?

All Yes, please.
Dodger This time I won't call out the action. Right. The party's going on.
Suddenly the Flying Sauceress arrives.

*Dodger rejoins the party. Watchdog, as the Flying Sauceress, "enters", searches,
finds the almanac, finds the formula, growls out the formula. All freeze. Watchdog reacts pleased. He mimes drawing the ray gun. The Prime Minister presses
the switch, the alarm rings. All move exaggeratedly and cry, "Tick, tock, tick,
tock". Watchdog panics. Sergeant Watchit walks forward and "arrests" him.
Cheers*

End of Optional Section

Suddenly the noise of the flying saucer is heard. All react

It's the real thing! Good luck, everyone. Try not to move a muscle!

Old Father Time exits to the main cog

*Watchdog enters his kennel. All position themselves and act out the party. The
hands of the clock-face should say 11.58. The saucer noise stops. Tension music*

At the clock-face window appears the Flying Sauceress

*No-one takes any notice of the Flying Sauceress. A bubble of party conversation
continues. Surreptitiously she enters the window in the clock-face and looks
around for the almanac. She spots it on the console and gingerly makes her way
towards it, making sure nobody sees her. She opens the almanac, turns a few
pages, then, wide-eyed with excitement, finds the "stop-time" formula. She gives
a quick look to check nobody is aware of her presence, then—*

Song 11C   MIRABILE DICTU (formula) [*reprise*]

Flying Sauceress (*singing in an audible whisper*)
                    Mirabile dictu orbe tum
                    Consistete et desinete nunc ipsum.

*There is a dramatic chord as everybody freezes, including the audience. Then
the noise of the main cog clicking to a halt is heard. The Flying Sauceress can
hardly believe her success. (N.B. The following section must not be played for
laughs. The audience must be given the chance to achieve a statue-like stillness
without being overtly tempted to laugh)*

It worked. I have stopped time. Even Big Ben has stopped. And every earthling is frozen still. Perhaps I should check for trickery. (*She puts down the
almanac and goes up to one or two of the frozen "victims" and peers at them,
giving the odd prod*) And now some of the smaller earthlings. (*She surveys,
at the actress's discretion, the audience, perhaps going into the auditorium
and peering at individuals. Eventually*) I am satisfied. They are all ready to
be fluenced.

*Tension music. Slowly and dramatically the Flying Sauceress produces her ray
gun and raises it, pointing at the characters on the stage. At the vital moment,*

the Prime Minister presses the alarm switch, which rings loudly. Everybody, including the audience, moves exaggeratedly and yells "Tick, tock, tick, tock". In addition, the main cog is heard starting again. The Flying Sauceress acts as planned. She panics, bewildered, on the spot, and drops her ray gun

Stop it! Stop it! Stay still! Stay still!

As planned, Sergeant Watchit approaches confidently

Sergeant Watchit (*taking her arm*) I arrest you, in ...

But the Flying Sauceress is too quick for him. She grabs his rifle and aims at him as she backs away

Flying Sauceress No, you don't arrest me. You keep your distance. And pick up my ray gun.

Nervously, Sergeant Watchit goes to pick up the ray gun. Suddenly, the Dinosaur makes a fierce noise, pushes through the crowd and confronts the Flying Sauceress

Aaaah! Get away. I'll fire!

The Dinosaur lunges forward and pushes the rifle into the air. (Optional: If the gun is practical, the Flying Sauceress could fire it as it points upwards. This may be considered disturbing for young audiences, though probably it would not upset them) The rifle drops, and the Flying Sauceress and the Dinosaur stalk each other. The others watch and shout encouragement. Suddenly the two grapple: then the Flying Sauceress escapes and dashes to the window of the clock-face

I *shall* stop time! I shall!

The Flying Sauceress jumps and grabs the little hand of Big Ben to stop it moving. For a couple of seconds she hangs there: then, very loudly, the chimes of Big Ben echo—"Ding, dong, ding, dong"

On the fourth clang (*of the introductory ones, not the main strike*) *she loses her grip and falls screaming to the ground outside*

Cheers. During the second set of introductory clangs: "Ding, dong, ding, dong", the Prime Minister speaks

Prime Minister It's midnight! A Happy New Year. Everybody.

The twelve clangs of midnight strike. Music joins them. Mrs Sparkle dashes to the calendar and turns it round. On it are written the words of "Auld Lang Syne". As the clangs ring out, all sing, encouraging the audience to join in

Song 12   AULD LANG SYNE

All   Should old acquaintance be forgot
                 And never brought to mind
                 Should auld acquaintance be forgot
                 For auld lang syne.

For auld lang syne, my dear
For auld lang syne
We'll take a cup of kindness yet
For auld lang syne.

Mrs Sparkle (*speaking*) Let's sing it again, everyone. Raise the horse's hoof.
All The horse's hoof?
Mrs Sparkle Yes. Raise the—(*encouraging the audience to join in*)—roof!
All (*singing*) Should old acquaintance be forgot
And never brought to mind
Should old acquaintance be forgot
For auld lang syne.

For auld lang syne, my dear
For auld lang syne
We'll take a cup of kindness yet
For auld lang syne.
Faster   For auld lang syne, my dear
For auld lang syne
We'll take a cup of kindness yet
For auld lang syne.

After the song, the music continues. Everybody turns, formally, as in a ceremony, towards the entrance to the main cog

Old Father Time enters, bringing with him the new Father Time—a child, dressed identically with Old Father Time—but no beard! Old Father Time leaves

The new Father Time slowly walks to the hour-glass which has run out, and turns it upside-down, to symbolize the start of another year. The Prime Minister picks up the almanac and presents it to the new Father Time. Mrs Sparkle shakes hands with the new Father Time and leads him to the cuckoo-clock kennel. From it comes Watchdog—a new, puppy Watchdog (played by a child), who bounds up to his master. The new Father Time winds him up

Prime Minister (*raising his glass*) The new Father Time.
All Father Time. (*They drink the toast*)

Song 12A   OLD FATHER TIME [*reprise*]

Half Chorus }
Old Father Time
Old Father Time
Old Father Time
Old Father Time
When you hear
  Big Ben chime
Hear Big Ben chime
Hear Big Ben chime
And you know it's
Father Time.

Half Chorus }
Checking his charts
Doing his sums
Making sure
Tomorrow comes
Day after day
Night after night
Making sure
They turn out right
He's been around
Since time's beginning

Making sure
The world keeps spinning
Big Ben will always chime
As long as there's a
Father Time.

All   The very first hallo
The very last good-bye
The moment when a chrys'lis
Becomes a butterfly
He's checking ev'ry second
As the clock ticks by
When Monday follows Sunday
He's the reason why.

Half }   Old Father Time
Chorus } Old Father Time
       Old Father Time
       Old Father Time
       When you hear
         Big Ben chime
       Hear Big Ben chime
       Hear Big Ben chime
       And you know it's
       Father
       Old Father Time
       Old Father Time
       Big Ben will always
         chime
       As long as there's a
       Father Time.

Half }   Checking his charts
Chorus } Doing his sums
       Making sure
       Tomorrow comes
       Day after day
       Night after night
       Making sure
       They turn out right
       He's been around
       Since time's beginning
       Making sure
       The world keeps spinning
       Big Ben will always chime
       As long as there's a
       Father Time
       Old Father Time
       Hear Big Ben chime
       Big Ben will always chime
       As long as there's a
       Father Time.

CURTAIN

In the Curtain Calls:

(1) The Dinosaur pulls on the Buskers' caravan, so we assume he will work for them from now on

(2) Dodger and Bodger carry placards saying "By Appointment to the Houses of Parliament"

Note: For walk-down or reprises, it is suggested that the songs "London, Wonderful London", "Two-Man Busker Band" and "Old Father Time" are the most suitable.

FURNITURE AND PROPERTY LIST

ACT I

SCENE 1

On stage: Big Ben cut-out
Westminster Hall (practical roof)
Sentry-box
Pillar-box
2 sets of railings
Mop and bucket (for **Mrs Sparkle**)
Rifle (for **Sergeant Watchit**)

Off stage: Cameras (**Tourists, Photographer**)
Gypsy caravan. *In it:* props and musical instruments, long trick spoon, eiderdown (**Dodger, Bodger**)

Personal: **Sergeant Watchit:** watch, trick phone in busby

SCENE 2

On stage: Large Big Ben clock-faces, with window and platform on one
Console with flashing lights, dials, knobs, microphone, headphones, pen, paper
Desk stool
Bed (grandfather clock shell) with trick hammer and alarm clock
Cuckoo-clock kennel
Large calendar on wall
Hourglass and sickle
Oil-can
Large red book (almanac)

Off stage: Tray with 5 cups of tea, saucers, spoons

Personal: **Watchdog:** watch/clock

SCENE 3

On stage: Flying saucer

Off stage: Ray gun (**Flying Sauceress**)

SCENE 4

On stage: As Scene 1, with buskers' caravan

SCENE 5

On stage: As Scene 2

Off stage: Mop and bucket (**Bodger**)
            Rifle (**Dodger**)

SCENE 6

On stage: As opening of Scene 1

Off stage: Ladder, bucket, leather (**Window Cleaner**)
            Sack (**Postman**)
            Broom (**Road Sweeper**)
            Large rock, 2 small rocks (**Stage Management**—brought on during "time
            change" when street scene is struck

ACT II

SCENE 1

On stage: As previous scene

Off stage: 5 spears (**Cavemen**)

SCENE 2

On stage: Westminster Hall and roof
            House cut-out
            Cottage cut-out

Off stage: Lantern, spear, keys on ring (**Beefeater**)
            5 lanterns (**Conspirators**)
            Powder barrels, fuse (**Conspirators**)
            Check water in **Mrs Sparkle**'s bucket

SCENE 3

On stage: Westminster Street as opening of Act I Scene I
            (Cottage and house cut-outs struck)

SCENE 4

Nil

SCENE 5

On stage: As Act I Scene 2, with addition of tables set with plates of party food,
            trays of drinks
            Bunting and flags as decorations
            Clock hands set at 11.50

Personal: **Sergeant Watchit**: handkerchief soaked in water

The following set plans were those used in the original production at the Queen's Theatre, Hornchurch, where flying facilities and trucks were available. While these are obvious advantages, the set changes that occur during the action can be achieved without them, provided the pieces are simply and lightly constructed.

PLAN 1

Act I Scenes, 1, 4, 6. Act II Scene 3.

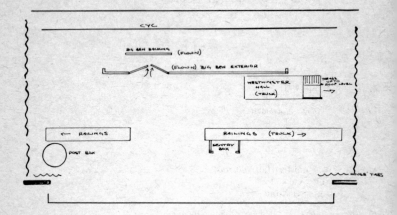

PLAN 2

Act I Scenes 2, 5. Act II Scene 5.

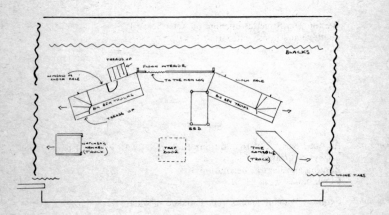

PLAN 3

Act I Scene 3.

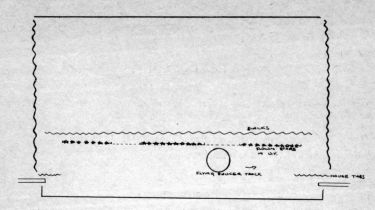

PLAN 4

Act I Scene 6a. Act II Scene 1.

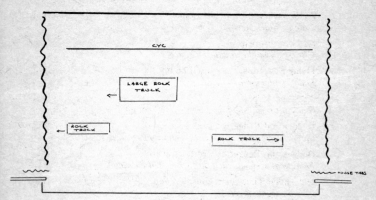

PLAN 5

Act II Scene 2.

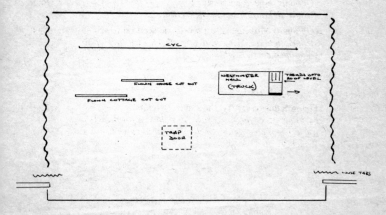

LIGHTING PLOT

Note: the following plot consists of cues essential to the action. These may be supplemented (for the songs, etc.) at the discretion of the Director

Property fittings required: flashing lights in console (Big Ben scene)
A street, inside Big Ben, in Space, front cloths

ACT I   Early morning

To open:	General overall lighting on street scene	
Cue 1	At end of "Old Father Time" song *Cross-fade to Big Ben lighting*	(Page 11)
Cue 2	**Old Father Time:** "... it gets pretty noisy" *Console lights flash*	(Page 17)
Cue 3	**Radio Voice:** "... intends to land" *Fade to Black-out*	(Page 18)
Cue 4	As Scene 3 opens *Ultra-violet light or spot on saucer*	(Page 18)
Cue 5	**Flying Sauceress:** "... you'll be my slaves" *Fade to Black-out*	(Page 20)
Cue 6	As Scene 4 opens *General overall lighting on street scene night*	(Page 20)
Cue 7	**Dodger** and **Bodger** go back to sleep *Slow change to dawn and early morning*	(Page 23)
Cue 8	**Dodger** and **Bodger** exit with caravan *Fade to Black-out, then up to Big Ben lighting*	(Page 23)
Cue 9	**Old Father Time** turns console knob *Console lights flash*	(Page 26)
Cue 10	**Radio Voice:** "... bring about world chaos" *Black-out, followed by spot on Big Ben (optional) and fade up to general overall morning light on street scene*	(Page 27)
Cue 11	(*Optional*) Speed up starts *Reduce lighting, bring in flicker-wheel*	(Page 29)
Cue 12	(*Optional*) Movement to prehistoric scene starts *Reduce lighting, bring in flicker-wheel, then fade up to cold, open overall lighting*	(Page 31)

ACT II   Day

To open:	As close of Act I	
Cue 13	**Flying Sauceress:** "To the saucer!" (exits) *Lighting effect for time-travel as before, with flicker-wheel if possible, followed by optional ultra-violet sequence*	(Page 43)

EFFECTS PLOT

ACT I

Cue 20	**Prime Minister** disappears *Flying saucer noise*	(Page 28)
Cue 21	At end of Formula (1) *Dramatic noise to increase speeding-up*	(Page 29)
Cue 22	At end of Formula (2) *Dramatic noise to accompany reverse action*	(Page 29)
Cue 23	At end of Formula (3) *Dramatic noise and ticking sound to accompany backward movement to prehistoric era*	(Page 31)

ACT II

Cue 24	**Dodger** and **Bodger** prepare to fight *Flying saucer approaching*	(Page 33)
Cue 25	**Flying Sauceress:** "To the saucer!" (exits) *Electronic time-travel noises, and ticking*	(Page 43)
Cue 26	**Old Father Time:** "... our pace through the past." *Noise increases*	(Page 45)
Cue 27	**Watchdog** and **Dinosaur** shrug *Flying saucer approaching*	(Page 47)
Cue 28	**Dinosaur** winds up Watchdog *Clockwork ratchet effect*	(Page 52)
Cue 29	At end of Formula *Time-travel noises*	(Page 53)
Cue 30	As Scene 4 opens *Flying saucer approaching and stopping*	(Page 54)
Cue 31	After **Flying Sauceress** exits *Flying saucer departing*	(Page 55)
Cue 32	**Prime Minister** presses switch *Alarm bell rings*	(Page 59)
Cue 33	(*Optional*) **Prime Minister** presses switch *Alarm bell rings*	(Page 60)
Cue 34	**Dodger:** "Back to normal then!" or At end of optional section *Flying saucer approaching and stopping*	(Page 60)
Cue 35	At end of Formula *Sound of main cog clicking to a halt*	(Page 60)
Cue 36	**Prime Minister** presses switch *Alarm bell rings. Main cog starts again*	(Page 61)
Cue 37	**Flying Sauceress** grabs Big Ben's little hand *Big Ben chimes and strikes twelve*	(Page 61)
Cue 38	**New Father Time** winds up puppy Watchdog *Clockwork ratchet effect*	(Page 62)

INCIDENTAL MUSIC PLOT

ACT I

Cue 19	**Dinosaur** comes round rock *Drum roll*	(Page 32)

ACT II

Cue 20	As Curtain rises *Tension music*	(Page 33)
Cue 21	**Bodger** and **Dodger:** "It was a dinosaur." *Music for Dinosaur's entrance*	(Page 34)
Cue 22	**Flying Sauceress:** "Think nasty thoughts." *Mood music, turning to Cavemen music*	(Page 35)
Cue 23	**Beefeater** starts to enter *Tension music*	(Page 46)
Cue 24	**Flying Sauceress:** "Think nasty thoughts." *Tension music*	(Page 48)
Cue 25	**Flying Sauceress** comes forward *Drum roll*	(Page 50)
Cue 26	**Guy Fawkes** lights fuse *Tension music*	(Page 51)
Cue 27	**Watchdog** enters with almanac *Fanfare*	(Page 51)
Cue 28	At end of Formula *Time-travel music*	(Page 53)
Cue 29	*Flying saucer arrives* *Tension music*	(Page 54)
Cue 30	At end of Formula *Dramatic chord*	(Page 60)
Cue 31	**Flying Sauceress:** "... ready to be fluenced." *Tension music*	(Page 60)

Printed in Great Britain by Butler & Tanner Ltd, Frome and London